GONE FISHIN'

ALSO BY WILLIAM G. TAPPLY

BRADY COYNE
MYSTERY NOVELS:

Death at Charity's Point

The Dutch Blue Error

Follow the Sharks

The Marine Corpse

Dead Meat

The Vulgar Boatman

A Void in Hearts

Dead Winter

Client Privilege

The Spotted Cats

Tight Lines

The Snake Eater

The Seventh Enemy

Close to the Bone

Cutter's Run

Muscle Memory

Scar Tissue

Past Tense

A Fine Line

Shadow of Death

OTHER NOVELS:

Thicker than Water
(with Linda Barlow)

First Light
(with Philip R. Craig)

Bitch Creek

BOOKS ON THE OUTDOORS:

Those Hours Spent Outdoors

Opening Day and Other Neuroses

Home Water Near and Far

Sportsman's Legacy

A Fly-Fishing Life

Bass Bug Fishing

Upland Days

Pocket Water

*The Orvis Guide to Fly
Fishing for Bass*

OTHER NONFICTION:

*The Elements of Mystery Fiction:
Writing the Modern Whodunit*

GONE
FISHIN'

Ruminations on

Fly Fishing

⟫━◆━⟪

WILLIAM G. TAPPLY

THE LYONS PRESS

Guilford, Connecticut

An imprint of The Globe Pequot Press

The Lyons Press is an imprint of The Globe Pequot Press.

10   9   8   7   6   5   4   3   2

Printed in the United States of America

Designed by Claire Zoghb

ISBN-13: 978-1-59228-889-2
ISBN-10: 1-59228-889-8

The Library of Congress has previously cataloged an earlier (hardcover) edition as follows:

Tapply, William G.
Gone fishin' : ruminations on fly fishing / by William G. Tapply.—1st ed.
p. cm.
ISBN-10: 1-59228-477-9 (trade cloth)
1. Fly fishing—Anecdotes. I. Title.
SH456.T35 2004
799.12'4—dc22
2004019045

DEDICATION

For James Babb, Joe Healy, John Likakis, Phil Monahan,

Art Scheck, Slaton White

CONTENTS

AUTHOR'S NOTE

M ost of these stories and essays appeared first on the back page of *American Angler* magazine in my "Reading the Currents" column. Some others were published as feature articles in that magazine or in one of its sisters—*Fly Tyer* and the now defunct *Warmwater Flyfishing*.

"Extreme Angling" and "Selective Perch" appeared in *Gray's Sporting Journal*.

"Twiggling" was published in *Field & Stream*.

"There Oughta Be a Law" and "Zen and the Art of Jiggering" are made public for the first time here.

ACKNOWLEDGMENTS

I've been thinking about how a kid who loved fishing ends up, all these years later, writing books about it. I mean, a lot of kids love fishing, but not many publish stories about it.

I was uniquely lucky to grow up with a fishing writer for a father. Or maybe he was a writing fisherman. He was very good at both, and even better at fatherhood. Almost as important to me were all the fishing writers/writing fishermen who were my father's friends and who didn't object when I tagged along with them. Naturally I read everything these men wrote, and quite naturally, their attitudes and approaches to fishing and writing made a deep impression on me.

The outdoors writers I liked to read—and they were also the men I liked to go fishing and hunting with—shared many similarities:

- they were storytellers
- they aimed for clarity and brevity
- they were humble
- they were funny
- they didn't settle for mediocrity
- they made it look easy.

I certainly want to acknowledge the contributions, direct and indirect, of all the book and magazine editors I've ever worked with. This book is dedicated to some of them, but there are many others. I'd list all their names if I wasn't afraid I'd leave somebody out.

My family and friends have supported me and encouraged me. Thanking them is hardly enough.

A fisherman has nothing to write about unless he spends time on the water, preferably with intelligent, observant, companionable partners. Andy, Bubba, Mike, Marshall, Vicki, Elliot, Steven, Jon, Randy, Art, Jeff, Art, Keith, Jason, Nick, Cliff, Tom, Joe, John, Phil, Joe, Phil, Blaine, Skip, Ted. . . . Lucky me.

Not to mention the professionals, the guides who row the boats and share their lore.

But I also need to acknowledge those special men of my father's generation, gone now, every one of them, who were my literary role models and my companions in the outdoors from the beginning: Harold F. Blaisdell, Corey Ford, Burton L. Spiller, Frank Woolner, Lee Wulff, and Ed Zern.

WILLIAM G. TAPPLY
HANCOCK, NEW HAMPSHIRE
AUGUST 2004

PROLOGUE

FIRST PRINCIPLES

One Saturday morning in the summer that I turned eight, my father peered across the breakfast table at me and said, "I guess you've been doing a lot of fishing lately, huh?"

That was the idyllic summer when the fishing bug sank its fangs into me and infected me for life. I was too young to work, too young for girls, but old enough to wander off by myself. So I fished every day, all day.

A muddy ten-acre pond lay over the hill behind our house, a four-minute walk for a kid who couldn't wait to get there. That pond was a magical place for an eight-year-old boy. It churned with warmwater life—frogs, turtles, dragonflies, muskrats, raccoons, minks, herons, ducks . . . and fish. Wondrous fish. Bluegills, punkinseeds, crappies, yellow perch, horned pout, pickerel, suckers, eels, and now and then a stunted largemouth bass.

"Yes, sir," I answered my father. "I love fishing."

He pushed himself away from the table. "Then it's time we got you a proper pole."

Now this was a strange notion. I already had my own fly rod, and for a clumsy kid I was pretty handy with it. It was a three-piece eight-foot Montague. Maybe I knew my Montague was a cheap, mass-produced stick, but the bamboo was a beautiful burnished bronze color, and my Pflueger Medalist reel had a musical click when I stripped line off it. My outfit was the envy of the neighborhood kids, most of whom used either Zebco spin-casting outfits or steel telescoping rods with old bait-casting reels taped to the handle.

I did a lot of digging in our vegetable garden that summer, and I found that with my sweet Montague fly rod I could lob a gob of worms pretty far out there without losing my bait. I didn't know it was called a roll cast. But I could do it.

So I already had a proper pole . . . although Dad's use of the word "pole" threw me. He was the one who insisted it was called a "rod."

But I knew better than to question my father. So I followed him into the woods out back, where he began narrowing his eyes at the clumps of saplings that grew there. After a lot of frowning and shaking his head, he selected a straight-growing poplar whip. It was about ten feet long and a little less than an inch thick at the base.

"What do you think?" he said.

I shrugged. "Looks okay to me."

He gave me his pocket knife, and I cut down the sapling, trimmed the leaves and twigs off it, and waved it in the air.

I handed it to him and he made casting motions with it. "Perfect," he said.

We peeled the bark off it and cut a foot off the tip, then took it home and rigged it with butcher's twine.

"There," Dad said. "Now you've got yourself a real fishing pole. Tie on some leader and a hook, make yourself a cork-stopper bobber, dig a can of worms, and go fishing."

What, I wondered, was wrong with my slick Montague bamboo fly rod? But I didn't ask and he didn't explain. So I obeyed my father and took my new pole fishing.

After that slender Montague, my poplar pole turned out to be heavy and stiff and clumsy. I couldn't roll cast with it for beans, but after a while I got so I could lob a bobber-and-worm far enough out there to catch perch and horned pout and derrick them in.

I stuck with that pole for about a week before I started sneaking out to my pond with my Montague fly rod. I never told Dad that I'd hidden our homemade poplar pole behind the woodpile. Luckily for me, he didn't ask how it was working, because I'd prepared a lie about how I busted it hauling in a big sucker, and I didn't like lying to my father. I felt guilty enough as it was. For some reason, it was important to him that I fish with that clunky pole we'd cut from the woods.

Pretty soon, when he saw that I was truly and forever hooked on fishing, Dad started taking me with him. We traveled all over New England—usually just the two of us, but sometimes with one of his adult fishing pals. We trolled streamers for landlocked salmon, we cast dry flies for trout and deerhair bugs for bass, and sometimes we used fly rods to drift worms in little woodland streams.

Dad and I went off fishing just about every weekend from April through September. That was my childhood. I was a lucky kid, and lucky me, I knew it.

In all that time, I don't recall my father ever once giving me a fishing lesson. He insisted I learn the Turle Knot (for tying a fly to a tippet) and the Blood Knot (for tying tippet to leader). After that, I was on my own. I learned to cast a fly the way I learned to lob a gob of worms out there—by trying and failing and trying it differently until it began to work better. I learned where fish hung out by putting my worm or fly in different places and letting the fish guide me.

I suspect Dad had to bite his tongue a thousand times. It would've been easy for him to say: "No, no. Do it this way." But he never did. We just went fishing together. He did it his way, and I did it mine, and you can be sure I watched him closely, because it was pretty obvious that his ways worked better than mine did.

A hundred times when I was growing up, and even years afterwards, I thought about asking my father why he'd insisted I fish with that poplar pole. But I never did. Maybe it was the guilt I never quite kicked about hiding the clumsy old thing behind the woodpile, though I have a strong suspicion that he knew exactly what I was doing.

Eventually I had three kids of my own. They all showed interest in fishing, and I was sorry that we didn't live in a house with a warmwater pond just over the hill out back. I never did cut them a poplar pole. Maybe I should have. But I did spend a lot of time in canoes with each of them, and I found myself biting my tongue and letting them fool around until they got the hang of it. I remembered the satisfaction I had felt whenever I figured something out for myself, and I didn't want to deprive my kids of that feeling.

Gradually, as I watched my own kids bumble and fumble, try and err, and finally grin and shout when they got it right, I figured I knew how Dad would've explained why he'd insisted I use that poplar pole. "First principles, my boy," he'd have said. "Begin at the beginning. Do it the hard way first. Try and err and figure it out for yourself. Don't skip any steps. You can't really appreciate where you are unless you know how you got there and where you came from."

Homemade poplar poles, butcher's twine, cork-stopper bobbers, gobs of garden worms, suckers, and eels—they're every angler's legacy, and if you skipped that part, well, when it's time to take a kid fishing, cut her a proper pole and resist the impulse to tell her how to use it. Let her begin at the beginning. You'll see what I'm talking about.

GONE FISHIN'

Part One:

THE FLY-FISHING PASSION

———✦———

For me fly-fishing was never a contemplative man's recreation. . . . If anything, fly-fishing was and is for me a constant state of excitement, and my attitude is best likened to that of a hound dog joyously baying in full, hot pursuit of its quarry.
VINCENT C. MARINARO, *A MODERN DRY-FLY CODE*

In the mornings we always looked and talked first. Then the sun grew warmer and before too long we would find some fish working.
NICK LYONS, *SPRING CREEK*

Then Dog-Nose starts pulling the fly back in with little yanks, letting the loops of rope fall round his feet, when all of a sudden the surface swells and that rope starts going back out again like a bolt of lightning.
CLIFF HAUPTMAN, *THE DOG-NOSE CHRONICLES*

CHAPTER ONE

EXTREME ANGLING

My son Mike made his first bungee jump in Wellington, on the North Island of New Zealand, when he was twenty. I had a father's unique and dubious privilege of watching my boy leap off an aqueduct, plummet two hundred feet toward a narrow silvery thread that was, in fact, a decent-sized trout stream, and then yo-yo in space for several minutes. He screamed when he jumped. It was a scream of enthusiasm, not terror. I think he yelled "Geronimo!"

I was the one feeling the terror. My mouth was too dry to scream as I watched my first-born, my only son, make that existential leap of faith with a rubber band around his ankles.

Mike rides bicycles up and down the sides of mountains and paddles kayaks through Class Three rapids. Hang gliding and sky diving and ice climbing are on his agenda. He admits he's kind of hooked on adrenaline.

He does a little fly fishing, too. He considered it a good antidote for his adrenaline overdoses. He calls fly fishing "the quiet sport." He read that somewhere.

I tell him: You want adrenaline? Try spotting a twenty-inch brown trout sipping ants three inches from the bank of a vodka-clear, slow-moving spring creek. Sneak up behind him one careful step at a time. When you get within sixty feet, go down on your knees and creep another twenty-five. Study that fish. Take his measure, find his rhythm, then make a couple of false casts to the side. You know you'll only get one shot. Blow that first cast and he's out of there. Take a deep breath. Go for it. Lay three feet of 6X tippet softly between that trout's eyes, and watch your size 20 foam ant drift down to him. When his nose pokes through the surface and your fly disappears in his maw and you know you've got to pause for a count of three before tightening on him . . . well, fly fishermen live for the rush.

Mike nods. He's done that. "But it's not the same," he says, and the way he looks at me, I know he's thinking that some day he'll be old like me and maybe his definition of a thrill will have ratcheted down that many notches.

People have died fly fishing, I remind him. They've been mauled by bears, zapped by lightning, dumped out of drift boats. Wade enough rivers and sooner or later you'll watch your life pass before your eyes.

Back in the early 1960s, the Kennebec River served as one of the main highways for Maine's paper industry. The loggers corralled the pulp logs behind big booms in the wide pool below the Wyman Dam in Bingham, and when they released them for their journey to the seacoast mills, a man with excellent balance could walk across the river without getting wet. Experienced Maine loggers, in fact, would dance over a raft of logs, prodding and poking at them with their steel pikes to keep them moving.

After the pulp run, there were always a few leftover logs twirling in the eddies along the bank. They were four feet long and nearly two feet in diameter, and after they'd been in the water for a while, they weighed half a ton. Now and then, if you happened to be standing in the river, a rogue pulp log might float past you, and you could stub your toe on one that had become waterlogged and sunk to the riverbed. Logging was one of the charms of the Kennebec, and of Maine in general, forty years ago.

When the loggers weren't running pulp on the Kennebec, big brown trout swirled and slashed at caddisflies in the three or four miles of river below the Wyman Dam. I liked to be there just about the time the sun sank behind the pines along the high banks. It was big water, a couple hundred yards wide. The currents were heavy, and the cobbled bottom was slick with two centuries worth of decomposed pine bark. The fish tended to rise out toward the middle, but I was young and strong, and I didn't mind wading up to my hips to reach them. I cast a bushy bivisible down and across and skittered it on a tight line past the noses of those big trout . . . speaking of adrenaline.

One July evening I got run over by a half-waterlogged rogue pulp log. I was facing downstream, finishing a long skittered cast, when it rammed me in the small of the back. It felt like getting hit by a slow-moving locomotive. The log knocked me off my feet and rolled over me, pushing my shoulders and head underwater, and for what seemed like a long time, but was probably only a few seconds, I tumbled and churned in the river with no sense of which was the surface and which was the bottom.

When my head bobbed up, I found myself careening downriver, and if I hadn't bumped into another drifting pulp log—or maybe it was the same one that had run me down—and grabbed desperately onto it and held on until I could find the riverbottom with my feet . . . well, I know I came as close to drowning that evening as I ever want to.

Adrenaline surged through my veins for the rest of the night. I felt no elation. It was all raw fear, and I didn't find it the slightest bit addictive.

Since then, I've harbored a healthy fear of rivers. I wade cautiously, and no matter where I am, some part of me insists on keeping an eye out for pulp logs.

Even watching one of my partners try something risky gives me a shot of that fear-adrenaline. I ask him *please* to be careful. I remind him that these are only fish we're after. Fly fishing is supposed to be fun— a quiet sport—not a test of your manhood. My partners generally ignore me. None of them has ever been run down by a pulp log.

So a few years ago when Andy Gill and I stood on the bank of the Henry's Fork a mile or so downstream from the Ashton Dam (and several miles downstream from the mob at the Railroad Ranch), it didn't surprise me when Andy pointed at the skinny island in the middle and said, "If we can get over there, we'll have a good shot at that nice run against the far bank."

The currents between where we were standing and that island appeared swift and deep. "It looks pretty good on this side," I said.

He shaded his eyes and pointed with his rod. "See there? Looks like a shelf? Get in there, wade diagonally up. We can make it."

"Maybe you can," I said. "Not me."

Andy shrugged and stepped into the water. I watched him go. Up to his knees. Hips. Waist. Chest. He held his rod over his head. It looked like was walking on tiptoes. Then his waist, his hips, his knees appeared, and he was sloshing up onto the island. He looked back, gave me a wave, and crossed to the other side and out of sight.

On my safe side of the river, a soft current flowed against the steep bank, and when I looked upstream, I spotted a black trout nose poking up beside an overhanging shrub.

The water was knee deep and it was comfortable wading. I worked my slow way upstream and quickly became focused on hunting for feeding fish, stalking them, and getting a float over them. I caught a couple of fat Henry's Fork rainbows and failed to catch several others. That pleasant, low-grade fly-fishing adrenaline was coursing through my veins, and until my left elbow hit the water when I pulled in my line, I didn't notice that as I'd moved upstream, the current had gradually grown heavier and the water deeper.

Now I was up to my belly button. I looked around. While I'd been intent on fishing, I seemed to have waded into a canyon. On my left, the bank rose almost straight up. It looked about a hundred feet high. Ahead of me, the waterline grew thick with bushes all the way to the dam.

Okay. It was time to get the hell out of there. I edged around a thorny shrub that grew out several feet over the surface. I had to go up on tiptoes, and when I did, the force of the current knocked me off balance. My foot slipped and water sloshed over the top of my waders. I grabbed a handful of shrub. A thorn the size of a wolf's fang rammed into my thumb, but I barely felt it. My adrenaline was surging now, and I held on, regained my balance, and pulled myself around the bush.

I scrambled out of the water and sat on the bank, breathing deeply and sucking my bloody thumb. I looked around. There was no path leading back along the bank to the car or in the other direction to the dam. Nothing but steep rocky slope and thorn bushes in both directions.

The only way out was straight up.

Well, it didn't look too bad. The bushes only grew along the bottom near the water. Just rocks and dirt between me and the top. I could do it.

I pulled off my waders and dumped the water out of them, then sat there for a few minutes, smoking a cigarette, sweating under the Idaho sun, plotting my route. It looked like there was a slightly diagonal course with rocky stair-steps all the way to the top.

The first five minutes went easily, even wearing neoprene waders over wet pants. Then I ran out of places to put my feet. I thought about climbing down to the river and wading back to the car. But one glance straight down settled that question. I was much higher than I'd expected, and the slope was considerably steeper looking down than it had seemed from below. If my foot slipped, I'd tumble down, smash against the rocks, crash through the thorn bushes, and land in four or five feet of dark, surging currents.

I thought of the nighttime climb Jon Voight made in *Deliverance*. That scene—in both the movie and the book—never failed to give me the willies.

I had no choice. I had to continue climbing. I reached up, laid my fly rod on top of a rock, felt around for handholds and footholds, and pulled myself up. Repeated the process, hand-and-foot rock climbing in wet neoprenes under that relentless, bodily-fluid-sucking sun.

After a while—I had no idea of how much time had passed—I found myself stymied on a narrow rocky shelf. I was drenched with sweat, gasping for breath in the dry air. My heart was hammering in my chest, and I thought: I am a middle-aged, out-of-shape man, a heart-attack or stroke candidate. I smoke cigarettes and eat red steaks and drink bourbon. Mounting a stepladder to change a light bulb always makes me dizzy.

I glanced down. The river looked black and deadly and very far away. It reminded me of looking down from that aqueduct in Wellington, New Zealand, knowing my son was about to jump. I pressed myself against the canyon wall, held on, and tried to catch my breath.

After a few minutes, I looked up. The rim of the canyon loomed high above me. The wall seemed to arch out over me. I didn't see how I could make it. I couldn't go up, and I couldn't go back down. I was stuck.

Something kept urging me to let go, to yell "Geronimo!" and push myself off, to take that existential leap. I actually found the idea tempting. It would solve my dilemma. I had to fight it.

Well, I wouldn't be telling this story if, in the end, I hadn't continued my climb to the top, pushing my rod ahead of me, clawing up that cliff, pausing to catch my breath, resisting the urge to look down, thinking only of the next place I could grip with my fingers and brace myself with my toes, blanking my mind of everything else.

When I got there, I lay on the ground for a long time waiting for the adrenaline to drain out of me. Both hands were bleeding, and my right knee throbbed where I must have banged it, though I didn't remember doing that.

After a while, I crawled back from the canyon rim and stood up. Except for the white-peaked Tetons in the distance, I seemed to be on the highest point of land in Idaho. The river was straight down. Two hundred feet, at least. As far down as Mike's bungee jump.

I shaded my eyes and spotted Andy. He was a tiny ant-figure down there near the tip of the island. I could see that he was bent forward like a heron, intent and predatory, casting his tight, graceful loops toward some rising trout he'd spotted near the far bank, fueled by little squirts of fly-fishing adrenaline, enjoying our quiet sport.

CHAPTER TWO

HEXED

My local trout stream is well known and heavily fished, and the fish all come from hatcheries, and if it weren't so, well, local, I'd probably not bother with it. But it's just a four-minute drive from my house, and I can visit it anytime the spirit moves me, which makes it pretty special.

Last June was dry and hot, and by the first of July, the water had dropped to mid-summer levels—lethal for trout, except maybe for a few smart ones that might find sanctuary at the bottom of the deep pools. I turned my angling attention to largemouth bass.

Then came two solid days of drenching rain. The sun came out at noon on the third day, and by five o'clock that afternoon, I couldn't resist. Ten minutes later, I was leaning my elbows on the bridge rail watching the currents swirl under me. The rain had brought the stream up to mid-season level, and it was running clear. A few dark caddisflies and tiny yellow mayflies fluttered over the water. I spotted no fish, but I remembered a spot about two miles upstream where an old milldam created a long deep pool. I'd spent many hours sitting quietly on the banks of the milldam pool watching herons and mallards and muskrats and Canada geese, and I'd never seen another fisherman there. I'd caught some fish from that pool, too. If any trout still lived in my stream, I figured, this would be the place. Maybe the rain had energized them and I'd find them looking up to the surface for some late-season mayflies.

Well, probably not. But at least I'd find some solitude on a pretty summer evening.

The streamside paths that we anglers had beaten down in April and May now grew chest-high in weeds and brush. Normally I'd go slow and pause beside every pool to watch the water. But on this afternoon, I had no faith in them. In my mind, the milldam pool was my only hope, and I found myself hurrying to get there, with visions of hatching mayflies and slurping trout dancing in my brain.

So I plowed through the underbrush, and a half-hour later I emerged at the bottom of the long pool at the dam. The current ran slow and deep along the far curving bank and disappeared around the corner upstream. The mud-bottomed, shallow near side by now had grown to lily pads and reeds.

Not a single fish was showing.

I squatted there and watched the water. The early-summer sun was low in the sky, and I figured I had an hour or so before I'd have to head back to my car. I'd neglected to stick a flashlight in my pocket, and I didn't want to end up clawing my way through the woods in the dark.

There were some spinners in the air, both tiny yellowish ones and a few big dark ones. Small dark caddisflies were fluttering over the water.

Then I saw widening rings way up where the stream bent out of sight, too far away to positively identify as a rising trout. But maybe.

The stream, I knew, narrowed and quickened at the head of the pool. That would be a good place to make my stand.

So I slogged a hundred yards upstream through the mud to a place where I could watch the entire length of the pool. I leaned my rod against a bush and sat. Pretty soon a muskrat emerged from the opposite bank with a clump of grass in his mouth. I watched him glide into his den, then emerge a few minutes later to fetch some more grass. Maybe he had made those rings.

Then a fish rose halfway down the pool. A trout, I was certain. If it came up again, I'd wade into position and try to catch it.

Ten minutes went by, and it didn't.

Maybe it wasn't a trout.

A goose and seven furry goslings paddled past me. Sphinx moths darted at some wildflower blossoms, looking like miniature humming-birds. Mr. Muskrat swam past my feet. Underwater, he looked like a monster brown trout.

It was all pretty cool. Sitting there on the bank of this long, slow pool on an early-summer evening, rising trout didn't seem very important.

The horizon was starting to show pink and orange when a truck materialized on the opposite bank down near the dam. A truck? I didn't know any road led to this pool hidden deep in the woods.

A man and a half-grown boy got out and walked to the water's edge. I sat still, hidden in the weeds, as disappointment bubbled into something like anger. It wasn't fair. I'd trekked this far through the woods with, admittedly, only the faint hope of finding rising trout, but with the confident expectation that I'd at least have the place to myself. I was feeling cursed. Snakebit. Hexed.

After a couple of minutes, the two interlopers went back to the truck, pulled on waders, rigged up fly rods, crossed the stream below the dam, and began casting into the tail of the pool. They were a hundred yards from me, but even in the fading light I saw the boy's rod suddenly arc and then the splash of a fish.

Soon the man's rod was bending, too.

I stayed where I was for a half hour, watching the two anglers catch fish while darkness crept out of the woods. It was bad enough they'd intruded on my private pool. But they also had the gall to catch trout from it.

I had no reason to stay. So I stood up and waded downstream through the mud to where the man and the boy were fishing.

The man waved. "Do anything?"

I shook my head. "I was waiting to see if something would show on the surface."

He nodded. "I figured. Saw you sitting there."

"What're you getting them on?"

"Little bucktails," he said. "We're waiting, too."

"Well," I said, "I gotta get back to my car. Good luck."

"Hey," he said. "You're not leaving?"

I nodded. "It's getting dark. I've got a long walk through the woods."

Just about then, the boy, who was up to his knees in the water, shouted, "Dad! I got one!" He was nine or ten, a skinny little kid, but he handled the fish expertly. He hand-landed it and showed it to his father before unhooking it and sliding it back.

"Way to go," I said to the boy. I nodded to the man. "Well, good luck."

"You can't leave," he said. "The hexes'll start hatching any minute."

"Hexes?" I said. "Here? You kidding?"

"Oh, yeah. It's awesome."

I shrugged. "I've got to get back to my car. I'm parked way down at the bridge."

"Stay," he said. "I'll drive you to your car. You got anything to match a hex hatch?"

I smiled. "Not hardly. Never knew we had *Hexagenia* in this stream. Never knew we had 'em in Massachusetts, for that matter."

He waded over to me, fumbled in his flybox, and handed me three dry flies. They had pale yellow bodies, white hackles tied parachute style, and tall white calftail wings. From head to tip of tail they measured about two inches. "You better tie one on while you can still see," he said.

I was tying on the fly when I heard the first slurp. By the time I looked up, there were a dozen or more dissipating rings on the surface of the pool and a scattering of huge, ungainly whitish mayflies flopping on the water.

And so I stayed into the darkness, fishing side-by-side with the man and his boy, and yes, we caught trout on those giant dry flies. Many trout, some of them bigger than any trout I'd ever caught on this stream.

When it petered out, he drove me back to my car at the bridge and waited there shining his headlights on me while I pulled off my waders, took down my rod, and stowed my gear in the trunk.

Lying in bed that night, I was thinking that I needed to start taking my stream more seriously. I shouldn't have to rely on the kindness of strangers to unlock its secrets.

I was just falling asleep when it occurred to me that I'd never asked the man and his son their names.

CHAPTER THREE

PAYING HOMAGE

Every year the weekend after Memorial Day, Marshall Dickman, Andy Gill, Jeff Christensen, and I spend four days in Roscoe, New York in the heart of the Catskills, where the fabled Beaverkill and Willowemoc Rivers meet at the Junction Pool.

Any angler with an ounce of piety throbbing in his veins venerates the sacred waters of the Beaverkill and Willowemoc, whether he fishes there or not. I've been guilty of referring to our annual Catskill trip as a "pilgrimage" to "hallowed waters." Marshall, Andy, Jeff, and I are not particularly devout men, but there is a certain religious fervor to our Catskill rituals.

We pull into Roscoe around noontime. We are itching to fish, but our solemn ceremonies must be observed. We drive straight to the Rockland House where our regular rooms are reserved for us. Jeff, who has come from another direction, is waiting on the porch. We register, dump our duffels, and head for town. We have cheeseburgers at the little hole-in-the-wall café, buy our licenses at the general store next door, visit Dennis at Catskill Flies to learn what's hatching and to buy a fresh spool of 6X, then head for the Hazel Bridge Pool.

We walk down to the water and squat beside it, let it run through our fingers, check it for depth and clarity, look for insects, watch for rising fish, debate hopes and possibilities. Then back to the car to pull on waders and rig up. Hazel Bridge is the most heavily fished pool on the Willowemoc. But we wouldn't think of starting anywhere else.

Each day goes the same familiar, comfortable way. Marshall, the early riser, bangs on our doors at six A.M. and leaves a mug of coffee outside. By six-thirty we're on the water. We fish until ten, recess for breakfast at the Roscoe Diner, then fish til four P.M., when we break for our afternoon nap. At six P.M. we take our stand at the Powerline Pool for whatever evening hatch might materialize. We fish into darkness, then head to Raimondo's for bourbon old-fashioneds and steak and potatoes. In bed at midnight. Up again at six for another day of it.

There is, obviously, an element of spirituality to all of this. But we feel pretty much the same way about all of our favorite waters, and we approach them all with reverence. We come to Roscoe every year because, when they're right, the Beaverkill and Willowemoc are fine dry-fly rivers. We come here to fish, and we want it to be good, and we're disappointed when it isn't. Worship has nothing to do with it.

When you plan a trip a year in advance, you take what the fishing gods decide to bestow upon you. The weekend after Memorial Day, we figure, is Prime Time. But as often as not we find the water too high or too low, the air too hot or too cold, the previous hatch gone by and the next one yet to arrive, the wind from the east, the barometer rising. The possibility of hitting it exactly right is what keeps us coming back.

Last year when we got to Hazel Bridge at two P.M. on Thursday afternoon, a brittle wind was howling directly downstream. We saw a smorgasbord of mayflies, including some big drakes, being blown horizontally, and we tried to buoy each other's spirits with the likelihood that toward evening the wind would drop, and spinners would fall to the water, and every fish in the river would rise to them.

It didn't happen. But by the second round of Raimondo's bourbon old-fashioneds that evening we'd found solace in the fact that the drakes were, after all, hatching. Surely tomorrow. . .

Friday dawned sunny and still, and we found some fish sipping spinners at daybreak. By the time we broke for breakfast, gray clouds had begun to gather, and when we left the Roscoe Diner, a soft mist was falling.

"Ah," whispered Andy. "A soft day. Olives." It sounded more like a prayer than a prediction.

If it was a prayer, the fishing gods answered it. Blue-winged olives were popping all over the Bend Pool. The fish were on them and we fished right through nap time.

At six P.M., per our ritual, we were standing on the bank over-looking the long, slow Powerline Pool. Wispy fog hovered over the glass-flat water. From where we stood, we could see a hundred yards in each direction. Not a dimple disturbed the surface.

"Huh," muttered Marshall. "Dead."

"Patience, my son," I said. "It'll happen."

Ten minutes passed. Then Andy pointed with his rod. "There."

Fifty yards upstream against the shadowy opposite bank I saw dissipating rings. "Your fish," I said to Andy.

"You go ahead," he said. "I've got to rebuild my leader."

I looked at Marshall and Jeff. They waved me to the water.

The fish came up two more times as I waded toward him, and I noticed that his dorsal fin, but not his nose, broke the surface. I spotted a few sulfurs popping up on the water. I knew what to do.

After I'd eased into position upstream and across from that fish, I knotted a foot of tippet onto the bend of my dry fly and tied a pheasant-tail nymph to it. The trout took it, first cast. As I played the fish, I glanced over my shoulder. Andy, Marshall, and Jeff had waded into the river below me.

By the time I released the trout—a nice sixteen-inch brown—rings were spreading all over the pool. I took a couple more fish on the nymph before they stopped eating it. Now scores of yellowish duns were drifting on the water. They weren't the tiny canary-yellow sulfurs that we usually found on the Railroad Pool. These were more tan than yellow and a size bigger, perfectly matched by the quill-bodied pale morning duns in my Montana spring-creek box.

It was not one of those blanket hatches where your fly gets lost in the crowd. There were just enough bugs to keep the fish eating, and the damp air kept them on the water. You could pick out a dun, watch it float down a trout's feeding lane, and see the nose lift and the bug disappear. After a couple of rises, you'd find the trout's rhythm, and if you dropped your fly precisely and if it drifted without drag, his nose would poke up and suck it in.

The fish ran fourteen to seventeen inches, most of them. Jeff landed one that measured nineteen. Big, lovely brown trout. They demanded a precise imitation and a drag-free presentation, and they refused to move to eat. But if you did everything right, they rewarded you.

It was utterly engrossing, a gift from the gods, about as perfect as an evening of dry-fly fishing can be, and we didn't even notice that the mist had become a soft, steady rain until it got too dark to see our flies on the water.

We had a couple of extra old-fashioneds at Raimondo's that night while the rain ran down the restaurant windows. We discussed the certainty that spinners would fall all over the Railroad Pool the next morning, and we savored the fact that we still had two more days of this heavenly fishing ahead of us.

It rained all night, and once the crack of thunder woke me up, but Saturday morning dawned cloudless and still. Perfect conditions for that spinnerfall.

We were the only car in the pullover by the Powerline Pool. We quickly tugged on our waders and rigged our rods, and then we strode down the path to get a look at the water.

None of us said anything for maybe five minutes.

The river was over its banks. It roared through the bushes, the color of cocoa, and I know Andy, Marshall, and Jeff were thinking what I was thinking: It wouldn't be fishable again for at least a week.

We laughed about it. Then we got breakfast at the Roscoe Diner, packed up, and drove home.

The fishing gods giveth and they taketh away. Amen.

CHAPTER FOUR

SEVEN FOR THE ROAD

"The literature of angling falls into two genres: the instructional and the devotional," wrote William Humphrey in his satirical little novel *My Moby Dick*. "The former is written by fishermen who write, the latter by writers who fish."

In the novel, Humphrey's narrator ("Bill") failed to find a fishing book that was both literate and instructive. Bill concluded that fishermen cannot write and writers cannot fish. It was a harsh commentary on the literature of angling.

No human activity other than sex and murder has spawned more books than fishing. Many of them seem to bear out the truth of Humphrey's observation. Luckily for those of us who love both fishing and reading, he exaggerated.

The last thing I throw into my carry-on bag when I'm off for a week of fishing is a book. It goes in last because I want it on top when I go rummaging for it. Also because the right book for a fishing trip is as important and difficult to choose as an emerger pattern for a spring-creek sulphur hatch.

I have stacks of unread fishing books, and if one of them should happen to written by John Gierach or Nick Lyons or Will Ryan or James Babb or Cliff Hauptman or Charles Waterman or a few other writers whom I trust, I'll bring it on a trip, confident that I won't be disappointed. Usually, however, I devour those guys' books as soon as I get them, so they're rarely in my unread stack.

I never pack a book I haven't already read. Like the trout I love to fish for, I'm selective. Any old book won't do for that important half-hour before I turn out the light at night or when I find myself riding out a storm in a cabin on a remote lake or in some grungy motel room. Spending time with a book I've never read is like inviting a guy I've never met to spend a week in a canoe with me. It might turn out well, but the odds are against it.

The fishing books that make it into my duffel bag are those that have already become my friends. I know I can count on them not to bore or irritate me.

Here, in no particular order, are the angling books that I keep packing with me for trips. I don't claim that these are the best books. I don't know what "best" means. But I do know entertaining writing and challenging thinking when I meet them. These are books that I have read many times with undiminished pleasure and interest, and I'm not done with them yet:

The Philosophical Fisherman by Harold F. Blaisdell (1969). It's dedicated "To all those sensible people who think fishing is ridiculous." That's a clue. I read this book for the first time when Blaisdell gave it to me the year it was published. Now it's tattered and dog-eared, and its pages are spattered with the question marks and exclamation points I've penciled on them over the years. It's one of those books that never fails to get my imagination whirling. It raises hard questions—about why fish strike, or don't strike, and, most perplexing, why we anglers think and behave the way we do. No matter how many times Blaisdell poses these questions, I find I still don't have pat answers.

A Modern Dry-Fly Code by Vincent C. Marinaro (1950). The word "revolutionary" is overused, but in the case of this book, it's on target. *Code* is about the discoveries that led to a revolution in dry-fly fishing for trout. Specifically, Marinaro discovered that trout eat midges and terrestrial insects and other "minutiae," and he devoted his life to learning how the angler might catch these challenging fish. Marinaro lived on the banks of the LeTort, the Pennsylvania limestone stream that he and Charlie Fox made famous. The LeTort was Marinaro's laboratory. He studied the stream's fussy trout—what they ate, what they refused to eat, how they behaved—and he wrote about what he observed. Everything we know today about fooling selective trout on slow-moving water with wispy tippets and tiny flies began here.

Now, half a century later, nothing in this book is outdated. Best of all for that half hour before the light goes out, it reads like a well-crafted story, with all the puzzles and clues and red herrings and dead ends and suspicious characters of a page-turning mystery.

What the Trout Said by Datus Proper (1982). This is another legitimately revolutionary book about trout flies—especially dry flies. "Angling books traditionally emphasize fly patterns," says Proper. "That is one reason why this one does the opposite and focuses on fly designs." The power of Proper's logic forces you to shift your entire understanding—the way Copernicus made us see the solar system and our place in it in a radically new way. Besides a wealth of eye-opening eavesdropping into what trout have to say about flies and insects, there's a lot of history, entomology, and technical stuff here. But Datus Proper is such an engaging narrator that the book reads like a conversation.

American Fly Fishing: A History by Paul Schullery (1987). Schullery says, "Calling fishing a hobby is like calling brain surgery a job." He is a writer who can fish and a fisherman who can write. He understands the passion. He's also a damn good historian. This book is full of lore that only Paul Schullery, who served as the executive director of the American Museum of Fly Fishing and has been honored both as an historian and as a writer, could have written. It's a book of anecdotes, personalities, and delicious tidbits of information—narrative history at its most compelling.

Spring Creek by Nick Lyons (1992). Once upon a time Nick Lyons found himself with a solid month to do nothing but fish in a heavenly Montana spring creek. It was full of big, selective trout, and the man who owned it chased away all trespassers. So Nick had it to himself. "I soon realized," he wrote, "that Spring Creek was the most interesting river I had ever fished or could imagine; and I learned that it was loaded with secrets that would take exceptional skill to learn." This book is about the creek and its fish and insects and the secrets it harbored. But it's mainly about the fisherman himself. Nick makes mistakes, and slowly, painfully, he learns. Nick Lyons, above all, reminds us of ourselves. Okay, any Nick Lyons book is good company. *Spring Creek* is my favorite.

The Dog-Nose Chronicles by Cliff Hauptman (1997). I've read *Dog-Nose* several times, and I can honestly say that I haven't learned a damn thing from it. For all I know, it's full of arcane lore and valuable angling tips, but I've always been too busy smiling and shaking my head at the clever puns and poems, admiring the dead-on narrative voice, and cringing at the biting satire to notice. Hauptman nails pretension wherever he finds it—fly fishermen, outdoor writers, magazine editors, literary pretenders, philosophers, guides, women, men, God . . . no one escapes. I know he gets me good. *Dog-Nose* is a laugh-out-loud book that seems to get funnier every time I read it.

My Moby Dick by William Humphrey (1978). With apologies to Ernest Hemingway, and despite my quarrel with Humphrey's generalization about fishing literature, this one is the best fishing novel ever written. Herman Melville's might have qualified, except a whale is a mammal. But if the white whale had been a trout—a very large trout living in a very small stream—and if a man's spirit became possessed with the idea of catching that trout, then you'd have Humphrey's story. *My Moby Dick* is at once a wry parody and a sharp commentary on the angling obsession. Every time I read it I find something new to ponder. That's the kind of book that keeps coming on trips with me.

William Humphrey, of course, was wrong. The literature of fly fishing is rich with good books, and his is one of them. But there are few great ones. Not many books on any subject can be read over and over with undiminished pleasure every time. On the subject of fishing I've found just these seven. They are my trip books.

Knowing I have a companionable old friend with me gives me something to look forward to besides the fishing. That is my definition of a great fishing book.

CHAPTER FIVE

THERE OUGHTA BE A LAW

The Church Pool is the most popular fly-fishing destination on the Farmington River, which is arguably New England's most popular trout stream. Toward the end of April when the Hendricksons start popping, the trick is to get there early, stake out a likely spot, and wait for it to happen.

The Church Pool has earned its popularity. It begins with a quick riffle, deepens into a boulder-strewn run, and then widens into a long, slow flat. The bridge at the top of the pool marks the beginning of the catch-and-release section of the Farmington known as the Trout Management Area. In the early season, other sections of the river are pounded by bait- and spin-fishermen, so the TMA—and the Church Pool in particular—is a mecca for fly fishermen. It's full of fish, and its hatches are heavy and predictable. When I find myself in a sociable frame of mind, the Church Pool is worth sharing.

By early afternoon on a late-April day a few years ago, the Hendricksons had petered out. I'd been standing in the same spot for almost four hours working over a delicious current seam that held a large pod of feeding trout—first with nymphs, then with emergers, then with high-riding duns, and finally with upstream wet flies for a persevering fish that looked like he might be eating drowned cripples. It was just frustrating enough to intensify my focus and to make each trout I landed gratifying, and I was only vaguely aware of the dozens of other anglers who had staked out their own spots in the Church Pool around me.

I realized that my bladder was full and my stomach was empty about the time I gave up on that last persnickety trout. When I reeled in and turned for shore, I noticed that the guy just upstream of me had a fish on. I watched him play it and release it, fiddle with his fly for a minute, then lob what appeared to be a weighted nymph into the current in front of him. He high-sticked it down maybe ten feet, and then he was hooked up again.

I looked around. Up and down the Church Pool, all those other anglers were casting. Several appeared to be using weighted nymphs. No other rods were bent.

The guy upstream of me landed that trout, fingered his fly, re-cast . . . and again he came up tight on a trout.

I couldn't resist. "Hey," I called to him. "What're you using?"

He looked up at me, grinned, and said something that was lost in the tumble of the water.

I wanted his answer.

So I started to wade through the shallow water near the bank to get closer to him.

And that's when I saw the white bellies. There must have been twenty dead trout slowly circling in the eddy just downstream of the guy.

"What'd you say you were using?" I asked again.

"Meal worms," he said. "On a size sixteen nymph hook. One small split shot, 4X tippet, dead-drifted near the bottom." He grinned. "Deadly."

"Deadly, for sure," I said. "You're killing them all." I picked up a dead trout, a nice fourteen-inch brown. "Look."

The guy shrugged. "I know. Can't help it. They keep swallowing my hook."

"But," I said, waving my hand around, "it's catch-and-release here. You can't do that."

"I can and I am, pal," he said. "I'm catching 'em and I'm releasing 'em, just like the law says."

I heard the hostility in his voice, but that was okay by me. I was feeling pretty hostile myself.

I waded closer to him so that if we raised our voices, we'd both know it was for emphasis, or in anger, not just to be heard over the rush of the water. "Maybe it's not illegal to gut-hook these trout with bait and rip out their throats when you unhook them," I said, "but that doesn't make it right."

"What's your problem?" he said. "I'm trying to catch some fish, just like you. Except it looks like I'm better at it. I'm not breaking any laws." He jabbed his finger at me. "So why don't you stop harassing me."

"It's my obligation to harass you," I said.

More than 2,500 years ago, Confucius argued that personal and community ethics—not laws—were the glue of civil societies. There were commonsense rules of conduct—the "spirit" behind every law—that governed civilized behavior. These rules did not need to be legislated, because most people instinctively understood them. They were enforced by individual conscience and peer pressure.

Communities began to collapse whenever people started to believe that they could do anything that wasn't specifically outlawed—and when others ignored their unethical behavior. Then, in order to keep societies intact, governments had to make more and more laws, train more and more lawyers, and hire more and more policemen. Proper behavior came to be defined as anything that wasn't illegal. Loopholes in the law were searched out and exploited until more laws were made to close them up. Gradually, acceptable—even admirable—behavior came to be defined as whatever you could get away with, including what might be specifically outlawed but difficult to enforce. Finally, civilizations fell apart under the weight of their laws and the impossibility of the state regulating all imaginable actions through legislation and enforcement.

Once when I was climbing down the steep path to the catch-and-release section of the Deerfield River, I paused to watch an angler hook, play, and net an eighteen- or nineteen-inch rainbow. He glanced around, then broke the trout's neck and stuffed it into the back of his vest.

When he got back to his truck, he found all four of his tires flat.

If Confucius was right, we're probably doomed. Any society that must specifically outlaw bait fishing in a catch-and-release trout stream acknowledges that its citizens will do anything that isn't specifically forbidden, while the rest of society turns a blind eye. It's honorable enough to be merely "law-abiding."

There's no need for personal ethics in a legalistic society. In fact, an ethical person is a loser. To compete successfully, to earn the admiration of one's peers, one does whatever he can get away with. When they make it illegal, find the loophole.

My examples concern fishing but you can find more important ones in the worlds of business and education and politics.

Not long ago striped bass were close to extinction. Since both sport and commercial fishermen refused to regulate themselves voluntarily, laws were enacted to limit the number of fish that could be kept and to require that any fish under a specified length must be returned to the water.

Because 99 percent of all stripers are under the minimum length, common sense—and the spirit of the laws—demands that fishermen use tackle and tactics that enable them to return the fish they catch unharmed. But the law does not forbid fishermen from using live bait (which stripers swallow) and big lures bristling with barbed treble hooks (which sink into the fish's eyes and rip apart their throats, tongues, and gills). And so law-abiding fishermen tear their hooks out of undersized stripers' stomachs and gullets and gills and eyes and throw their bleeding and mortally wounded catch back into the ocean, righteous in their knowledge that they have obeyed the law.

It will take increasingly more laws and cops to protect striped bass and trout—and children, and minorities, and people who are sick, elderly, poor, and defenseless.

If that bait fisherman I met in the Church Pool is typical, then it's obvious we can't depend on ethics.

But I will continue to harass guys like that. I hope you will, too. You can unscrew the valve stem of a truck tire with the forceps you use to unhook your trout so they can be returned unharmed to the water.

CHAPTER SIX

———◆———

COMING UNSTUCK

I t was noontime that pretty Tuesday in September, and I was sitting on the sofa watching television when Vicki came into the room and stood squarely in front of me. "For heaven's sake," she said "why don't you go fishing or something."

"Fishing?" I said. "What good would that do?" I waved my hand for her to move. "I can't see the TV."

"I never thought the purpose of fishing was to do good," she said. "You like fishing. You should do something you like to do, that's all."

"What right do I have," I said, "to do something I like to do?"

She rolled her eyes.

"You want me out of your hair," I said. "That's it, isn't it?"

"Sure," she said. "That's a good way to look at it." She sat down beside me. "All you've done for the past week is watch the news and play solitaire on your computer. You're stuck, sweetie. I wish you'd get unstuck. Go fishing."

I shrugged. "I don't feel like fishing."

"Boy," she said. "That's a first."

"This whole thing," I said, waving the back of my hand at the television, "is a first."

Somebody on the television was interviewing the mayor. In the background, rescue teams were swarming over the mountains of rubble where the airplanes had crashed into the tall buildings. The mayor was saying that the best revenge would be for all of us to keep on doing whatever we do. We should live our lives fully and defiantly. That would show the evil bastards that they hadn't won.

"You believe that?" I asked Vicki.

She shrugged. "Kinda glib, I think. But essentially true."

"You think if I went fishing, the bastards would notice?"

"No," she said. "But I would." She kissed me and stood up. "You would, too," she added, and then she went back to her desk.

After Vicki left the room, I thought about fishing as my moral obligation, my patriotic duty. It was a different way to think about fishing.

I thought about getting out of Vicki's hair, too, and it occurred to me that if I went fishing, it might reassure her, at least, that life did in fact go on. Perhaps that was my duty as her spouse.

I couldn't imagine going trout fishing. Too far to travel. Too complicated. Too engrossing. I didn't have the energy to match hatches, tie knots, interpret riseforms, read currents. I didn't feel like concentrating on anything.

Okay, dig some worms, I thought. Go to the millpond, sit on the bank, watch a bobber. Dragonflies would perch on my rod tip, bullfrogs would grump in the lily pads, herons would highstep in the shallows, migrating warblers would flit in the bushes, and bluegills and horned pout would make my bobber jiggle and dance. It would be like when I was a boy, when my whole world was a quiet millpond on a pretty September afternoon.

In the end, I took a box of panfish flies and a spool of 3X tippet and one of my cheap old glass fly rods. I didn't have the energy to dig worms.

My millpond is a five-minute drive from my house. The dam dates to the industrial revolution, and it backs the river up for several miles. When I was a kid, this was one of the dirtiest rivers in all of New England. On any given day it would run crimson or turquoise or vile yellow from the dyes and other chemicals the textile mills dumped into it.

Since they cleaned it up, it has become a decent panfish and largemouth river. Taking care of our rivers is one of the good things we do. We Americans make plenty of mistakes, but we know how to clean up after ourselves.

I parked in the pulloff beside the pond, and, as I always do when I go fishing, I got out of the car and walked down to check out the water. The pond looked like a bomb crater. It was lower than I'd ever seen it. Sunken trees and rocks and waterlogged brushpiles that were usually hidden under the surface poked up, and the mud banks that stretched out from the normal waterline were bare and still wet. I figured they'd opened some gates in the dam downstream this morning.

Then something swirled beside one of the rocks, and a switch clicked in my brain. I went back to the car, got my gear out of the back seat, and rigged up. I tied on a Turck's Tarantula, a buggy-looking thing made of deerhair and rubber legs. It was just the right size—small enough to fit in a bluegill's mouth, big enough to entice a largemouth. I stuck the flybox in one shirt pocket and the spool of tippet in the other.

My sneakers squished in the wet mud as I walked to the edge of the water. I false cast a couple of times, the old Shakespeare glass flexing slow and pleasant, and dropped the Tarantula beside the rock where I'd seen the swirl. First cast, a hand-sized bluegill. Two casts later, another one from the other side of the same rock.

I moved clockwise, one step at a time, covering the water, probing whatever structure presented itself, and every few casts something or other hit my bug. I caught a crappie the size of a dessert plate, a foot-long yellow perch, a six-inch largemouth, a dozen bluegills. Across the pond, where the early-autumn swamp maples were turning crimson and orange, a pair of mallards splashed in. There were deer tracks in the mud, damselflies in the air, and the mingled aromas of wet mud and rotting weeds in my nostrils, and it all reminded me of countless September afternoons when I was a boy on the bank of some millpond watching a bobber and trying to come to grips with the fact that my endless summer was actually ending.

Something caught my eye. It was less than a swirl. A ripple of nervous water, a fin briefly breaking the surface—a good-sized fish of some kind alongside a stump that was sticking up out toward the middle of the pond off the tip of a muddy point, normally an underwater bar. Aha.

I bit off my soggy, bluegill-chewed Turck's Tarantula and tied on a bass-sized deerhair bug. Then I eased my way out to the tip of the point. The mud was softer here, and it sucked at my sneakers.

It was a long cast from the end of the point to the stump where I'd seen the nervous water, but it felt good to throw a long line with the old glass rod, to feel its creaky flex right down to my hand, to wait that extra second for the line to straighten out behind me, and it wasn't until I tried to lift my foot to move one step closer that I realized I was stuck.

I was nearly up to my knees in mud the consistency of half-set cement. When I tried to pull one leg out, it drove the other one in deeper, and then I was in over my knees, half way to my crotch. I was *really* stuck.

It wasn't like quicksand. I'd been in quicksand. In this mud, as long as I remained still, I sank in no deeper. So I stood there up to my thighs in mud and made a few casts out toward the stump, thinking,

This isn't such a bad place to be, stuck or not stuck, with water in front of me and a fly rod in my hand.

Sooner or later, of course, if you find yourself stuck, you have to try to get unstuck. So I reeled in, hooked the bass bug in the keeper ring, and tossed the rod toward the shore. And then I lay on my back and made oars of my arms and rowed backward in the mud, and slowly, slowly, my legs pulled free, leaving my sneakers and socks behind. Then I rolled over and belly-crawled back to where I could stand up.

I found my rod and started clumping back to my car. That's when I noticed that another car had pulled in beside mine. A pair of teenagers, a boy and a girl, were sitting in the front seat with the windows open. I could see that they were smiling at me. I figured they'd been watching my entire performance.

The boy leaned his head out the window and yelled, "Hey, mister! Any luck?" And the two of them laughed and laughed.

I was covered from head to toe with greasy, smelly black mud. It was in my hair, up my nose, under my shirt, inside my boxers, and I thought: I wish Vicki could see me now. She'd laugh.

I gave the two kids a thumbs-up. And then, for the first time in a week, I laughed, too, and I finally felt myself come unstuck.

Part Two:

TACTICS AND
TRICKS

———❖———

*If you can avoid drag, you have at least an outside
chance of a fish, no matter what other errors you make.*
DATUS PROPER, *WHAT THE TROUT SAID*

*. . . I quit fishing entirely, content to lay aside my
tackle. Stretching myself prone on the bank with my
eyes not more than one foot from the water, I
beguiled the time by watching a small trout nearby
feeding in the manner of his brothers.*
VINCENT C. MARINARO, *A MODERN DRY-FLY CODE*

*The very narrowness of the channel would demand a cast
of pinpoint accuracy . . . and the very stillness of the
surface meant that my fly must fall upon it so unnoticeably
as to seem not to have fallen but to have hatched. . . .*
WILLIAM HUMPHREY, *MY MOBY DICK*

CHAPTER SEVEN

—◆—

PLAYING GUNS

I learned the importance of stealth as a young teenager when I discovered that native brook trout lived in the little stream that meandered through the woods not far from my house in eastern Massachusetts. I'd spotted them churning around in a riffle one autumn afternoon, as pretty as the maple leaves that drifted on the water, all orange and crimson and green, easily identified by the ivory edges on their pectoral fins.

I went back in April with my fiberglass fly rod and a can of worms. I waded downstream, drifting my bait through every likely hole, and I covered nearly a mile of the stream without getting a single bite. It wasn't until I stepped into the riffle at the head of a delicious shaded pool and saw the wakes skittering away that I figured it out.

In that little brook, I realized, trout learned to survive by fleeing first and asking questions later. As far as they were concerned, I was a heron or a mink or a kingfisher. Those wild trout lived on the edge all the time.

The next time I visited that brook, I emulated the minks and the herons. I fished my way upstream, not down, and I stayed out of the water. I wore drab clothing and I moved slowly, crouched over, watching my shadow, being careful where I placed my foot. I stopped often and looked hard, and I didn't drop my worm into the water without a purpose. I knelt in the mud and stuck my rod through the bushes. Mosquitoes chomped on me. I got wet. Briars scratched my face. And I managed to catch a few of those lovely little trout.

I'd heard anglers more experienced than me say, "You can't catch anything if you don't have your line in the water." Now that struck me as misleading advice. On that little brook, where food was scarce and enemies were abundant, I spent more time hunting and stalking than I did actually fishing. Most of the time, my line was not in the water. I learned that the stealthier I was, the more trout I'd catch. When I tried them on flies, I learned that they'd eat almost anything provided I hadn't spooked them with my approach and I took pains to make a soft, accurate cast.

I grew up in a little rural town surrounded by farms and woods and swamps and brooks. In those postwar days (I mean World War II), before television, before Little League, and before computers, we kids had to invent our own fun.

Most afternoons after school we played "guns," a variation on hide-and-seek in which the winner "shot" the loser with his cap pistol or water gun or even just his index finger. It was a game of hiding in the woods, of stalking and pursuing, of seeing without being seen. We played no roles. There were no cowboys and Indians, no GIs and Nazis, no good guys and bad guys. It was each boy for himself. A game of guns might last all afternoon as six or eight of us crept through the woods, hiding under bushes, hunkering behind boulders, trying to get a fair bead on somebody before he spotted us. Then we'd aim our gun and yell, "Bang! Gotcha."

Guns was a game that came naturally to prepubescent boys. Hiding and stalking required no instruction. No grownups showed us how to do it, or organized it for us, or encouraged us to play. We all could do it, and none of us ever tired of it.

Playing guns taught me how to move so slowly as to seem motionless. I could creep through the autumn woods without cracking a twig or crunching leaves. When I slithered on my belly from tree to tree, I was both hunter and hunted, and I knew, even if I couldn't articulate it, that I had tapped into something atavistic and important.

In those days, nobody saw anything dangerous or disturbing about a bunch of boys slinking through the woods trying to shoot each other with make-believe guns. When we got a little older we stalked squirrels and rabbits with real guns, single-shot .22 rifles and .410 shotguns, and nobody saw anything dangerous or disturbing about that, either.

Now, of course, the town where I grew up is a densely populated suburb of Boston. Hunting is outlawed there, and skulking through the woods is considered unhealthy and unnatural, and any boy who likes to play guns visits the child psychologist weekly.

I still play guns. Now I use a fly rod instead of a cap pistol, and I stalk trout instead of my neighborhood pals. When I creep along the bank of a stream or kneel motionless behind a bush, scanning the surface for the pinprick rise of a feeding fish and squinting into the water through my polarized glasses for the white wink of a trout's mouth or the anomalous wave of a tail or the fish-shaped shadow against the bottom, that primitive feeling is there, as strong as ever. It absolutely convinces me that the urge to stalk and pursue lives in my genes. It explains why trolling and stillfishing and blind long-distance casting does not fulfill me the way hunting for stream trout does.

I still get a kick out of slinking along a little woodsy brook, "reading" the water and dropping a fly onto a riffle or into a likely hole for a trout that does not suspect I am there. But whenever it's possible, I look for fish. I locate a target trout, and then I stalk him, just the way I used to stalk Bobby Allen and Richie Kinsman through the woods forty-five years ago.

If he spots me before I fool him into eating my fly, the trout wins. If I manage to catch him, I shout, "Gotcha!"

I still love to play guns.

I approached my first visit to the little spring creek with apprehension. I'd heard how smart these trout were, and I wasn't sure I was up to the challenge.

I'd been standing in one place for several minutes, casting futilely to a trout that seemed to be sipping Pale Morning Duns, when I glanced down and saw three large rainbows finning in the currents not ten feet directly downstream from me. They were feeding regularly, and I quickly understood that whenever I moved my feet I kicked up nymphs and scuds for them, inadvertently performing a San Juan Shuffle.

What struck me, of course, was the fact that they could see me clearly. There I stood, in plain sight, waving my rod around and shuffling my feet, and not only did they not spook but they had actually approached me.

Those heavily fished spring creek trout accepted fishermen as part of their natural environment. They'd figured out that we weren't herons or minks. If they spooked every time a man with a fly rod stepped into the water, they'd go hungry. For those trout, survival meant ignoring two-legged intruders and being wary of what they ate. They'd learned to recognize the difference between a natural drift and one that dragged, and between a Pale Morning Dun mayfly and a bunch of feathers and fur tied onto a hook. Catching these trout required a different kind of stealth.

I thought I had it figured out. Predators stalk the banks of pristine wilderness streams, and trout survive by evading them. But in lightly fished water, where food is often scarce, survival also means grabbing a bug—any bug—quickly before it gets away.

In heavily fished waters, trout get used to two-legged intruders in neoprene waders. But they learn to be picky about what they eat.

Of course, it's really more complicated than that, for which I am grateful. If it weren't complicated, it wouldn't be so much fun.

I've found wild little brook trout in hidden mountain streams and beaver ponds sipping hatching mayflies as selectively as Henry's Fork rainbows, and so intent on it that they continued rising even when my careless step sent waves rolling across the pool.

Bighorn River trout, on the other hand, are pounded all summer. They've seen hundreds of driftboats and waving fly rods. Yet in shallow water, where their old survival instincts remind them that they are especially vulnerable to predators, they can be as skittish as any wilderness brookie. To catch them you must practice stealth—locate them from afar, approach them from downstream, wear drab clothing, crouch low, tie on a close imitation of what they're eating, lay slender tippets directly between their eyes, achieve perfectly drag-free floats. The overhead flash of a fly line or the splash of a leader butt blows them up, and even a passing drift boat in mid-river puts them down.

Catching trout always demands stealth of one kind or another. More than once the flitting shadow of a sparrow has spooked a trout I'd been stalking for fifteen minutes. You've either got to sneak up on trout without them knowing it, or you've got to fool them with clever imitations and natural presentations of what they're eating. Most often, you've got to do both.

It's hunting. It's playing guns. But we've been practicing stealth since we slithered out of the slime, so it's no wonder we never get tired of it.

CHAPTER EIGHT

BANK SHOTS

Bill and I picked our lunch site for the shade of the lonely cottonwood, the gurgle of the river, and the upstream view. The brown-and-yellow Montana plains rolled off to distant horizons all around us, and the sky was as big and blue and cloudless as advertised. But we had eyes only for the water. As we munched our sandwiches and sipped our Cokes, we watched about a dozen trout sticking their noses out of a shadowy fifty-yard band of shallow slick water that flowed inside the main current against the high bank.

We had each of those trout located. They were all holding within a yard of the bank. We knew they were big by their unhurried, no-nonsense riseforms. No flashy attention-getting boil, no splash, no noise—just those big noses poking rhythmically out of the water. After lunch we'd work our way upstream and take turns picking them off, one by one.

We pointed our rod tips at them and tried to guess their sizes and what fly they might like to eat and whether they were browns or rainbows. It was fun, just watching them and knowing they were there, and we were in no hurry. Bill assured me that the fish weren't going anywhere, and neither were we.

Then we heard voices. "Uh-oh," Bill muttered.

Three men with fly rods materialized on the high bank. They gazed across the river and talked about it for a minute. Then they skidded down the steep slope, sloshed through the calf-deep water—just upstream from where our lineup of big trout had been feasting—waded purposefully out to their waists, and went to work.

They stood shoulder-to-shoulder, lobbed big neon-pink strike indicators into the heavy current in front of them, high-sticked them along with their rod tips, lifted and lobbed again. It looked monotonous.

Our bank-sipping trout, of course, had disappeared.

The three nymph anglers stuck to it for nearly an hour and caught a few smallish fish before they reeled in, splashed back to shore, and wandered away.

Bill and I waited, and less than a half hour later, big noses began to poke up in the flatwater that we'd been watching.

Bill stood up. "Okay, Grandfather," he said. "Let's go bank shooting."

Bill Rohrbacher is a guide, and he goes bank shooting every day he's got a client who's willing to catch fewer trout and have more fun doing it. When he realized that I found it as addictive as he did, he decided I was okay even if I had gone to college, and we became friends and fishing partners. He began to call me "Grandfather" (I'm a full ten years older, though he's much trout-wiser), and he told me that all his friends call him Bubba.

Bubba's an uncanny bank shooter. I'm still learning. I'll know I've got it right when I don't spook any of them.

We spent most of the afternoon with those bank sippers, working our slow way upstream from fish to fish, taking turns. We waded on our knees some of the time, keeping a low profile and stalking them from directly downstream. We used 6X tippets and black deerhair beetles. We made short casts—twenty or thirty feet, no more—and we kept our false casts off to the side to prevent shadows and flashes from spooking the fish. Perfect casts—laying just the tippet "between their eyes" and dropping the fly two or three feet upstream so it would drift onto their noses—usually brought a strike. Imperfect casts—a couple inches off to one side or the other—produced nothing.

We didn't exactly pick them off one by one. We never do. We spooked a couple of them by sloppy wading. I dropped the butt of my leader on top of one, and in that foot-deep water he "blew up" (Bill's term) with a swirling explosion.

One trout spurned Bill's repeated offerings. He cursed it inventively, changed flies several times, then knelt on the riverbottom, pressed his palms together, bowed deeply, and said, "Okay, God bless you, dammit."

We raised a few that we failed to hook, or hooked briefly before they came unbuttoned. One—we guessed he would've gone twenty inches—busted me off.

We ended up landing five of them, three eighteen-inch browns and two slightly larger rainbows. Well, in the interest of full disclosure, Bill landed four of them, although he and I don't really think of it that way.

On a famous Montana river where eastern sports such as I like to brag about thirty-fish days, I was replete. I'd raised several large trout, hooked a few, landed one, and lost another. Each encounter was memorable.

It was a helluva afternoon.

Afterwards we talked about the three guys who plowed through a lineup of the biggest, most catchable fish in the river. "It don't surprise me," said Bubba. "Most guys, they figure big trout want the big water and that big trout make big splashes when they rise. Of course, they're wrong." He scratched his beard and grinned. "It's ironic, you know? When people fish from driftboats, they cast as close to shore as they can. But when they're on foot, for some reason they ignore the banks and wade in up to their bellybuttons."

In most rivers, Bill has taught me, big trout actually seem to prefer the flat, shallow water that flows against the bank inside the heavier currents. Sheltered under overhanging brush or tight against boulders, they lie there in comfort and tilt up at their leisure to sip whatever comes their way.

Rarely do we find small trout in the skinny bankside water where they would be most vulnerable to predators. Maybe when trout reach a certain size they start believing they're too big to interest herons and ospreys. Or maybe they think they're too smart and survival-tuned to get caught.

They are pretty smart. But they can be caught.

Concentrating on the narrow bands of soft water near the banks has saved me from being overwhelmed by the size and complexity of big waters from Maine to Montana. Bubba has taught me how to step into unfamiliar rivers for the first time and consistently find feeding fish. I simply ignore the bigness of strange waters and concentrate on those rivers-within-rivers that flow softly against the banks.

Small trout waters are just like big ones, except, if you'll excuse me, for their size. They contain the same complexity of currents, the same combinations of holding water and barren water, as their out-sized counterparts. On western spring creeks and eastern freestone streams alike, I concentrate my attention on the soft inside cushions of water. Trout like to lie with their sides almost brushing the bank, smack against logjams or under weed patties or in the shadows of overhanging bushes or tufts of grass, sometimes in water barely deep enough to cover their backs. Their delicate riseforms are easy to miss. They look like fingertips poking quickly out of the water.

These are usually large fish. They didn't grow big by ignoring hints of danger. They have not forgotten about herons. In slow-moving skinny water, it doesn't take much to spook feeding trout. Sharp eyes, delicate, precise casting, long, fine tippets, neutral-colored shirts and hats, and old-fashioned stealth are keys to stalking bank feeders.

In the smooth, slack water next to the bank, trout have plenty of time to think before they eat. Anything tied to a leader tippet must behave naturally. It cannot drag, however slightly, and it must pass directly through the fish's feeding lanes, because they will not move far to eat.

If we hunt hard enough, Bubba and I can usually find a few bank sippers eating off the surface even when the river looks dead. We've had fine dry-fly fishing at midday while all the other anglers on the river were sitting on the bank waiting for the next hatch.

Bank sippers tend to be opportunistic feeders. Rarely is fly pattern the important variable in catching bank-feeding trout, although it's fun how they can sometimes be maddeningly picky. Usually, it's all in the approach and the presentation.

Once you spot a bank sipper, pinning down its location is easy, because you have several points of reference—eight inches out and a foot down from that trailing branch, for example, or right on the inside seam of that tiny lick of current flowing around a boulder. Wear good polarized sunglasses, because in shallow water you can often see the ghosty shape of your target finning just under the surface. Get low, creep close, and position yourself for a straight upstream cast. Make your first shot count. Drop your fly two or three feet above him. Watch him as he spots it, flicks his tail, drifts under it, turns, lifts his snout, and shows you his open white mouth. Resist the impulse to strike too early, if you can.

Bank shooting combines the best parts of hunting and fishing, which is probably why it's the kind of angling I have grown to love the most. Each fish is a challenge. It's head to head, just that single trout and

I alone on the river—or, even better, with Bubba kibitzing at my elbow. I don't mind spending half an hour trying to catch it.

No two bank sippers are quite alike. Each one offers its particular challenge, and no matter which of us wins, the hunt provides me with another memory. It's money in the bank.

CHAPTER NINE

TWIGGLING

In my family, oh, half a century ago, the fishing season opened sometime in April with a phone call from Charley Watkins, who owned some housekeeping cabins on Sebago Lake in Maine. The old guy was quite deaf, which convinced him that he had to yell in order to be heard. If I was in the room when Dad answered Charley's call, I had no trouble following Charley's end of the conversation.

"SHE'S CRACKED OPEN, MR. TAPPLY," he would scream as Dad held the phone away from his ear. "ICE WENT OUT THIS MORNIN'. YOU BOYS BETTER GIT YERSELVES ON UP HERE. I GOT CABIN THREE WAITIN' FOR YOU."

Dad would yell, "WE'LL BE THERE FRIDAY NIGHT," and Charley would scream, "WHAT'S THAT YOU SAY?" Dad would repeat himself, his face growing redder and redder, until Charley finally hollered, "WELL, SOMETHIN'S WRONG WITH OUR CONNECTION, BUT I'LL BE EXPECTIN' YOU AND THE BOYS ON FRIDAY NIGHT, OKAY?"

Dad was the eastern Massachusetts landlocked-salmon Paul Revere, so after he hung up with Charley Watkins, he phoned the alert to Tom Craven and the Putnam brothers and Gorham Cross and his other fishing partners, and to each of them he gave his own high-decibel imitation of Charley Watkins. "SEBAGO'S CRACKED OPEN," he'd yell. "TIME TO GO FISHING AGAIN."

I sat patiently at the kitchen table, and when Dad finished his round of calls, he'd look at me. "You can come, if you want," he'd say.

Of course I wanted.

Landlocked salmon were legendary gamefish for a young boy, and I knew all about them. *Salmo salar sebago,* they were called, after the lake where we fished for them and where the rod-and-reel record, a twenty-two-and-a-half-pounder, was taken in 1907.

Once upon a time, Maine salmon lakes conjured up the same magical images for fly fishermen as famous Rocky Mountain trout rivers do today. Sebago, of course. Moosehead and Rangeley, Chesuncook and Seboomook, Parmachenee and Aziscohos, Mattawamkeag and Pemadumcook, Machias and Sysladobsis, West Grand and Big.

Landlocked salmon, like their anadromous Atlantic brethren, spawn in rivers. In fact, according to the theory, they began as Atlantic salmon running up what once were great salmon rivers— the Kennebec and Penobscot and others that drained the hundreds of lakes in Maine. But when the dams of the nineteenth century blocked the salmons' route back to the sea, they were forced to adapt to life in fresh water. They became landlocked.

At one point, biologists believed that landlocks were a species distinct from Atlantics. The difference, they said, was the shape of a single inconsequential bone. Nowadays, biologists have reverted to their original assumption—that landlocks and Atlantics are the same species.

Landlocked salmon fishing meant trolling streamers and bucktails sporting evocative names for a young boy—Grey Ghost and Warden's Worry and General MacArthur, Supervisor and Dark Edson Tiger and Nine-Three—over the points and dropoffs along Sebago's rock-strewn shoreline, around the Dingley Islands, and back and forth across the mouth of the Songo River. Those classic Maine streamer flies, according to the theory, imitated smelt, which swarmed in the shallows after ice-out preparatory to spawning in the feeder streams.

We rigged our bamboo fly rods with a Dark Tiger—always a Dark Tiger, although to my eye it looked nothing like a smelt—on the end of a long leader, with one of those classic landlocked patterns for a dropper. Dad claimed that ninety percent of his salmon came to the Tiger, but since landing a single salmon was always considered a triumph, we never caught enough fish to constitute a valid sampling.

Wind, which was often accompanied by cold rain, made for prime salmon trolling. Presumably, salmon lost their caution when the water was choppy, and they lurked near the surface looking for streamer flies. Windy days were, in fact, the norm for southern Maine in mid-April. When it blew, we dragged short floating lines along the windward shoreline where, according to the theory, the smelt got churned around by the sloshing surf, making them disoriented and vulnerable to predatory salmon.

When Sebago lay flat and glassy, we let out the entire flyline, Dad cut back the motor to its lowest non-stalling speed, and I sprawled on my bow seat, tilted up my face, and closed my eyes to the warmth of the sun. I don't recall ever getting a strike under flat-calm conditions. On such a day we'd wait for the wind to come up and trigger the four o'clock flurry. It often happened just that way.

It was like duck hunting: The worst conditions made the best fishing. A salmon troller was supposed to welcome misery.

Wind was the key—but not just any wind. We believed utterly in
the old New England folklore:

> When the wind is from the east,
> That's when salmon bite the least.
> When the wind is from the north,
> That's when fishermen set not forth.
> When the wind is from the west,
> That's when salmon bite the best.
> And when the wind is from the south,
> It blows the bait to the salmon's mouth.

For the first few hours of the first morning of the new season,
regardless of the conditions, I leaned tensely forward in my bow
seat, facing back to where my flyline trailed out and disappeared
behind the boat. I gripped my rod in both hands, expectant and
alert, ready for whatever kind of salmon strike might come—a "tip-
dipper" or a "rod-bouncer" or a "reel-screecher" or any of several
subtle variations of each.

But actual strikes were rare, and when my high-strung boy's
anticipation dulled, which it did rather quickly, I cut a stick, wedged
it in the gunnels, and braced my rod against it, on the well-docu-
mented principle that salmon were most likely to strike when you
least expected it. Then I allowed my mind to wander on the hypnotic
thrum of Dad's two-horse Evinrude, and I tried to recall those rare
but magical times in the short memory of a young angler when my
tip *had* dipped and my rod *had* bounced and my reel *had* screeched
and far behind us a silvery arc *had* exploded from the gray corrugated
water that, only a few days earlier, had been ice.

When it actually happened, it was always unexpected. The rod
bucked against the gunnel stick, then bent acutely, and the reel zizzed,
and as I fumbled for it, a salmon leaped far out behind the boat.

Sometimes there was no leap. Then we had a delicious mystery on the end of the line—a "squaretail," maybe, a genuine native Maine brook trout, which often ran four or five pounds in Sebago. Or a lake trout—we called them "togue"—those deep-water char that ventured to the surface briefly after ice-out, when the water was as cold on top as it was down deep.

Or maybe a really big salmon who didn't feel like jumping.

Mostly, though, I remember long, cold, rainy April days on the lake in a leaky rowboat with my father. His attention never seemed to wander. When I got restless, he told me stories, and I understood that if you already had a storehouse full of fishing memories, it was easy to pay attention.

"Try twiggling," he'd tell me. "Give it some action." And he'd pick up his rod and saw it back and forth a few times, as if to convince me that he had faith in his own advice.

So I'd saw my rod back and forth for a while, and although I don't remember ever actually having a salmon strike when I was holding my rod in my hands, I never doubted the magical properties of twiggling.

A century ago, landlocked salmon grew wild in just about every cold-water lake in Maine. They shared the water with brook trout and lake trout, but those species all seemed to coexist in stable balance. As long as the lake supported a healthy population of smelt, salmon prospered.

By the time I started going with my father, white perch and smallmouth bass had begun their invasion of the salmon lakes. Both species were voracious, aggressive, and adaptable. They reproduced sinfully and spread rapidly. They ate smelt—and landlocked salmon fry, too, no doubt—and wild salmon populations were on the decline.

Dad remembered the good old days. I just caught a backward glance at them.

Nowadays, the state of Maine aggressively sustains landlocked salmon populations by stocking hatchery-bred fish. They raise them right on the banks of Grand Lake Stream, and on the Hatchery Pool the stockers sip Hendricksons off the surface just like trout. They leap like, well, like salmon when they're hooked, and even when you know they were born in cement tanks and were nourished with pellets, it's fun to catch them.

On a choppy, wet April afternoon on Sebago shortly after the ice goes out, they'll still grab a Dark Tiger trolled behind a leaky rowboat. Your tip will dip, your rod will bounce, your reel will screech, and far behind the boat, a silvery arc will explode from the gray water.

If the fishing is slow, try twiggling.

CHAPTER TEN

—◆—

BASS BUGGING FOR TROUT

"**Y**ou guys up for something different?" said Aaron, our guide, as we loaded our gear into his truck for our evening trek.

Jon Kolb, my partner, didn't hesitate. "Absolutely."

"Depends," said I, betraying the difference between us.

"No guarantees," said Aaron, "but the conditions are perfect."

If you'd asked me, I would've said the conditions were rotten for trout fishing, and most especially for an evening of top-water fishing on a small farm pond. The stiff breeze would riffle the water and the heavy gray cloud cover would make sight-fishing impossible.

"What've you got in mind?" said Jon.

"Greased muddlers," said Aaron. "Cast 'em out there and chug 'em back across the surface. The fish go berserk. It can be wild."

"Like bass bugging," I said.

"Sure," said Aaron. "Except it's for trout. I hope you don't mind, but we're unlikely to catch anything under eighteen or twenty inches."

"Oh, that's okay," said Jon.

The idea of using deerhair bass bugs and bass-bugging techniques for trout should have occurred to me a hundred times over the years. The fact that it never did reveals the power of the conventional wisdom on the differences between bass and trout.

Bass, I believed, were opportunistic, hot-tempered, and impetuous. They ate anything that struck them as edible. They reacted to motion and noise. They could be angered or teased or otherwise seduced into striking a lure that resembled nothing in nature. Whether a bass bug happened to resemble a frog or a minnow was irrelevant. It was all in the gurgle, ploop, and pop.

Trout, on the other hand, were selective and cerebral and wary. They scrutinized the tidbits of nourishment they found in the water and ate cautiously. The size, shape, color, and behavior of potential food all mattered to squinty-eyed trout. To catch them, you had to fool them with a fly that looked and behaved like what they were eating at the time.

On occasion I encountered some bass—smallmouths, mostly—that behaved remarkably like trout. They sipped mayflies off a river's surface, and they seemed to prefer flies that looked like the insects that were on the water.

Over the years, I've met trout that behaved exactly like bass, too—trout that turned and slashed reflexively when I plopped a big hopper behind them, trout that rolled on a streamer the instant it hit the water, trout that followed and hit a dry fly when I dragged it back across the surface to recast, stillwater trout that crashed damselfly imitations. But my assumptions about trout psychology prevented me from recognizing what I was seeing.

When I was a teenager, my father and I often fished Vermont's Otter Creek near Middlebury College with Harold Blaisdell. Our favorite technique for those big rainbows and browns was to skitter large, high-floating dry flies down and across the current on a tight line. The trout chased them and swirled at them, missed them and hit them, and we busted off more than we landed.

I recall thinking that those trout acted a lot like the predatory largemouths and smallmouths I liked to catch on bass bugs. But Harold and Dad explained to me that our skittering dry flies imitated the caddisflies we saw skating on the water. You caught trout by imitating what they were eating, of course.

Every year for a quarter of a century Dad and I floated the pastoral Pine River near his home in New Hampshire a couple of times every season. We took turns steering his little thirteen-foot Grumman from the stern and casting from the bow. The only fly we ever used was a Cooper Bug, which is a trout-sized version of the famous Devil Bug that Orley Tuttle invented to catch bass (which should have been a clue). We roll-cast the Cooper Bug against the banks and into riffles and current tongues, twitched it down and across, and those pretty little Pine River brookies gobbled it.

We figured those trout ate our Cooper Bugs because they imitated terrestrials—the beetles, ants, crickets, and inchworms that plopped off the banks into the water and twitched and struggled in their alien environment. Maybe. Maybe not.

Dorman, my Inuit guide, introduced me to catching trophy Labrador brook trout on deerhair mice. The technique was identical to skittering dry flies and twitching Cooper Bugs—cast it to the other side of the stream, hold the rod high, and wake it across the current. Those monster brookies came slashing and crashing, furious and frenzied and seemingly mindless—more like pike, or bass, than trout.

"They think it's a lemming," explained Dorman when I commented on their decidedly un-troutlike behavior.

I've caught trout by twitching big hopper and cicada patterns at times of the year and in waters where none of those naturals was evident, and my only explanation has been that the fish "remembered" how nourishing the real things were. My flies imitated the image of a specific food item in the trouts' memory, I figured.

It didn't occur to me that at least sometimes, under some conditions, big trout could be just as impetuous as bass, or that they might go for any big mouthful of something that looked alive, or that bass-bugging methods might be a good way to catch them.

So as we bumped up the dirt road to the old farm pond that summer evening, it was natural that I'd ask Aaron what our greased-up muddlers would be imitating, that the trout would want to eat them.

"Imitate?" said Aaron. "Wounded minnow? Frog? Mouse? Dragonfly? Take your pick. Personally, I don't think they imitate anything. I think the noise and the motion just triggers some subconscious predatory impulse. These fish aren't thinking. They're reacting."

"Like bass," I said.

"Exactly."

When Aaron parked his pickup truck beside the little pond, I saw that its surface was gray and wind-riffled and altogether uninviting.

"Ahh," he said. "Perfect."

We strung our 8-weights and climbed onto the berm that the farmer had bulldozed to dam the brook that fed the pond, and I was still tying on a size 6 marabou muddler when I heard Jon whoop.

When I looked up, I saw a hole in the water. "What was *that*?" I yelled.

"Trout," said Aaron matter-of-factly. "Big one." To Jon he said, "Keep it coming . . . he's still after it . . . there!"

There was a tremendous *ker-slosh* and Jon's rod bent double. Then a rainbow trout shot into the air. It was at least two feet long and it looked like a tarpon, arced high over the little pond. When it hit the water, Jon's rod went limp and so did he.

"Omigod," he mumbled. "Did you see that?"

I did. It didn't make tying on a fly any easier.

For the next couple of hours Jon and I double-hauled big floating flies and jerked them back across the riffly surface of the pond, and big trout kept chasing them. They swirled, splashed, struck, and we missed some and hooked some and busted some off, and when it was finally too dark to see, we'd each landed four or five fat rainbows, most of which measured well over twenty inches long.

We chugged floating bugs over trout ponds several other times that week and I drew some tentative conclusions about the method:

1. It worked best when a breeze riffled the water and the sky was overcast. The activity slowed down noticeably when only one of those conditions prevailed; flat water under a bright sky produced nothing.
2. A slow, steady chugging retrieve induced more strikes than either a twitch-pause-twitch or a series of long, fast strips.
3. Jon and I had about the same number of strikes, but at first he hooked a higher percentage of fish than I did. When I changed to a smaller fly, my success rate improved. We concluded that a size 8 streamer hook, making a fly about an inch and a half long, was optimal.
4. Pattern or color made no apparent difference, but the most productive flies floated low on the water and pushed a wake. Jon used something called a Turck's Tarantula and I stuck with a muddler. We fingered fly floatant into our flies, and when they became waterlogged, we squeezed them dry.
5. This was not a method to use on waters where big fish didn't live. The smallest fish we caught measured seventeen

inches. On the other hand, according to Aaron, taking into account the fish we landed, those we hooked and lost, and the crashing strikes that failed to produce hookups, we had probably sparked interest from the biggest fish in the ponds.

Would we have caught as many fish using streamers? Maybe. Would we have had as much fun? Absolutely not.

CHAPTER ELEVEN

———◈———

THE GULPER RULES

I made my first cast to a Hebgen Lake gulper on a misty August morning many years ago, when I was much younger and knew way more about fly fishing than I do today. Nowadays I'm discovering all the things I don't know. Back then I knew everything.

So when I dropped my fly dead center in the widening rings of the big trout's riseform, I said, "Bull's-eye!" and glanced smugly at Bob Lamm, who was paddling along beside me in his float tube.

"Lousy cast," he said.

"Are you kidding?" I said. "That happened to be a perfect cast."

He chuckled. "Not if you want to catch that fish. Think about it."

Think? Rings pocked the glassy skin of the lake all around us. Half a dozen trout swirled within a thirty-foot cast of our tubes, poking up their noses to gobble the freshly hatched *Callibaetis* duns that were trying to dry their wings in the moist early-morning air.

They were obviously worthy trout. Seventeen to twenty inches,

Bob had promised, with the chance of bigger ones. And they were eating mayflies off the surface. Who could think? But this was my debut at gulper fishing and Bob was an old hand at it. I might've been a know-it-all but I wasn't dumb. So I tried to think.

After a minute, I said, "Okay. I get it. They're cruising."

"Right," said Bob. "So the worst place to cast is into the bull's-eye. You can't always tell where they're going. But it's for dang sure that the one place they ain't gonna be is where they just were. See, it's just the opposite of stream fishing. In moving water, the fish hold a lie and wait for the food to come floating to them. In still water, the bugs stay put, so the fish've gotta go get 'em. Rule Number Two in gulperin': Take your best guess and lead your trout."

"Number Two? I must've missed Rule Number One."

"You've gotta be in the right place at the right time," he snorted. "Rule One. I thought that was self-evident."

"Sure," I said. "I knew that."

A minute later Bob pointed with his rod. "There. That one's really gulpin'. Try him."

The fish was coming fast at eleven o'clock, moving straight toward me. Every three or four feet he lifted his head, cut a wake across the water, and sucked in several bugs. I could actually hear him slurp. Piece of cake.

I dropped my No. 16 parachute Adams twelve feet ahead of him, directly in his path, and held my breath. I stared at my fly's smoke-colored wing with one eye and watched the trout close the distance with the other. A collision course.

"Eat!" I whispered.

He veered away a scant yard before he arrived at my fly.

"Quick," whispered Bob. "Again!"

I lifted, false cast once, laid it out there. But the fish had gone down.

"Guess I spooked him," I said.

"Doubt it. He's a trout, that's all. He goes where he wants."

Which, I was to learn, was Rule Number Three, also known as the Catch-22 of gulper fishing.

Bob and I had launched our float tubes before daybreak. Mist hovered over Hebgen, shrouding the shoreline and the snow-topped peaks beyond. Soon enough the August sun would burn off the fog but in the dawn's half-light the air was cool and liquid, and the water's surface lay as flat and dark as a mug of camp coffee. It was eerie and silent and beautiful, and suspended out there half in and half out of the water, neither of us cared to violate the tranquility of the place by talking. So we paddled in comfortable and companionable silence across the narrow Madison Arm toward the steeply banked north shore. That's where the rainbows would come out to play, Bob said.

The lake was scummy with a smorgasbord of midges and Trico spinners and dead caddisflies, and only an occasional isolated swirl disturbed its surface. "Do we chase them?" I asked Bob.

He shook his head. "They're just foolin' around until the *Callibaetis* come off. Sometimes they get up and really munch them Tricos but mostly before it's light enough to fish for 'em. That little box of Adams parachutes is all you need for gulpers."

By the time we had finned halfway across the lake, a scattering of speckled duns had begun to pop to the surface. A few trout rose, more duns appeared, and suddenly the hatch was underway. Soon I could count a dozen rising trout within casting distance of my float tube.

I'd waited my whole life for a crack at these Hebgen Lake gulpers. I could wait no longer.

That's when I began to strip line off my reel and aim for the bull's-eye. And that's when I learned the three rules of gulper fishing.

We were there and the trout were gulping. We'd already obeyed Rule Number One. So I attempted to apply rules Two and Three.

An occasional fish exhibited that classic "gulping" behavior I'd read about. They'd wake across the surface with their dorsal fins showing and their mouths chomping audibly, submerge briefly, then come up again to gluttonize some more. Those trout, I noticed, did not move predictably. Some of them plowed steadily in a straight line before dropping out of sight. Some zigzagged, some took sharp right-angle turns, some moved in a long curve.

Most of the trout, actually, did not "gulp." They rose to the surface, took a bite or two, then descended, only to rise again six or eight feet away.

There were always plenty of fish to cast to and I tried them all. I'd spot a rising trout, guess his route, cast ahead of him, and wait, tense and poised. It was exhilarating. It was heart-stopping. It didn't take me long to understand why gulper fishing was addictive.

It was also humbling. Invariably my target trout chose a route other than the one I'd chosen for him and rose somewhere other than where my fly sat. In an hour I raised just one fish—not the one I was casting to. No surprise that I left my fly in its jaw. Some hotshot.

By then Bob had taken three fat rainbows. Eighteen or nineteen inches, I estimated.

"Should I change flies?" I finally asked him.

"I'm using the same one you are."

"Maybe I should go down to 6X."

"I'm using 4X, myself," he said.

"I'm going to watch you."

I paddled over and parked my tube beside him. A trout swirled forty feet away at two o'clock.

"Watch and learn," Bob murmured. He false cast once and dropped his fly thirty feet away at three o'clock.

"Why'd you cast there?" I said.

"That's where he's headed," he grunted, straining forward in his tube.

A black snout lifted and Bob's fly disappeared. "There. See that?"

"Of course I see that," I muttered.

He played, netted, and released the rainbow, a quadruplet of his previous three. He blew on his fly and arched his eyebrows at me.

"Okay," I said. "So there's a trick to it."

He shrugged. "Not really. Not a trick. I'm not sure I can explain it but I usually seem to know where they're headed. I couldn't tell you exactly how, but there's a head and a tail and a curve to their body and a movement to their fins and a shape to their swirl, and maybe something else I can't explain, and it all somehow computes. All I can say is it's more than guessing and less than knowing. If you try to analyze it, you'll never get it." He shrugged. "You just gotta clear out your head and go with it."

"Zen," I mumbled.

"I don't know about that," Bob said. "You don't catch 'em all. They're trout, after all. Grant 'em plenty of free will."

When I finally started to get it, it did feel like Zen, or something equally mysterious. I flicked my fly to the left and a little beyond the swirl of one particular trout, and for no reason that I could explain, I was absolutely confident I had it right. And I was not at all surprised when his nose lifted and his mouth clamped down on my little Adams.

Around mid-morning it started to slow down, so we paddled back across the lake to the shallower southern side. There we found brown trout gulping leftover *Callibaetis* duns among the reeds. Like the rainbows on the other side of Hebgen, these browns averaged seventeen or eighteen inches. Like the rainbows, too, they exercised plenty of free will, and it required all of my Zen powers to get it right, to clear my head so I could "see" their route, and to intercept a couple of them.

Before the wind came up, as it does every day in Montana, and blew the bugs and our float tubes off the water, I got it wrong plenty of times, too. Rule Number Three. Trout are trout, after all. If they weren't, why would we bother trying so hard to catch them?

CHAPTER TWELVE

ZEN AND THE ART OF JIGGERING

I've never truly thought of ice fishing as *fishing,* any more than water skiing is *skiing.* And it's nothing whatsoever like fly fishing. It can be fun, I suppose. But it's not the same.

So last January when Ted Williams invited me to his favorite pond for a day of fishing, I looked out my window at our frozen New England world and said, "*Ice* fishing, you mean."

"Not hardly," he said. "Jiggering." He paused. "Jiggering is to ice fishing as dry-fly fishing is to heaving Rapalas with your Zebco."

Since I had no idea what the hell *that* was supposed to mean, I decided I better go find out. . .

I've been slogging through calf-deep snow for twenty minutes, dogging Ted's heels, following an old logging trail through pine-and-oak woods, then across a long sloping meadow where deer and coyote tracks crisscross. Wilson, Ted's Brittany, has already flushed and chased a grouse and made serious game on a nuthatch.

Now, finally, the snow-sheeted pond lies before us. It could be a flat winter field except for a couple of tiltmen and their snowmobiles over toward the far shore. Wilson spots them and heads in their direction.

Yellow perch live in virtually every body of fresh water that freezes in the winter. But Ted has picked this one, an hour's drive from our homes and a mile from the nearest plowed road. When I ask him why, he fixes me with his "stupid question" stare.

He whacks the ice experimentally with the business end of his chisel, studies the low, gray January sky, and sniffs the air. "Could turn into a good jiggering day," he mutters. "If we're lucky, we'll get some snow out of it."

"They bite better in the snow, huh?"

This is my first day of jiggering. I am the apprentice, the cub, the novice, the greenhorn, the rookie, and I am playing the role to the hilt. Ted knows his part by heart, too. He has given no indication that I am—or ever will be—welcomed into the elite, however disreputable and curmudgeonly, fraternity of jiggermen.

"Clouds," he says, "are good. Snow or rain is best."

I do not ask the obvious question: How do yellow perch, in twenty feet of water under snow-covered ice, know when it's raining or snowing? Ted, I feel certain, would shrug and say, "They know," meaning, again: "Stupid question."

He marches out onto the ice which, it turns out, the wind has swept almost bare. I slip-slide along behind him. Suddenly, at some spot undifferentiated from any other on the hundred-acre pond, he stops and, one-handed, chops a hole. He takes only six or eight well-placed whacks with his heavy five-foot ice chisel before water and slush well up.

"Plenty of ice," he says.

"How much is plenty?"

"Inch. Less than that, you've got shuffle ice. Shuffle ice, you don't stand too near your hole when you spud it. Less than shuffle ice, it's prayer ice."

"So how much have we got today?" I ask, somewhat prayerfully.

"Five inches. Way too much for easy spudding."

I've noticed that a long rawhide thong droops around Ted's neck. A wooden handle is attached to each end, and sticking out of each handle is what looks like the pointed end of a ten-penny nail. I think I know what this contraption is for but I point to it anyway. "Ever fallen in?"

"All jiggermen fall in," he says.

Oh. Another stupid question.

"After last time," he adds, "I made myself this thing."

"Does it work?"

He shrugs. "I expect one of these days we'll find out."

I have already decided that jiggermen are fanatics.

Ted lays his chisel on the ice and begins to rig up. Wilson returns from his visit with the tiltmen and sits beside him.

Ted has already given me a quick vocabulary lesson. I know he's worried that if we run into another jiggerman today, I'll embarrass him by saying something stupid.

"In the first place," he told me as we rode over in his truck, "it's *jiggering,* not jigging. And don't *ever* call it 'ice fishing.' Ice fishing is what those damn tiltmen with their spring-loaded tipups do, and that ain't any kind of fishing. It's trapping."

Now he's threading his line through the guides of his "jiggerstick." All jiggermen make their own jiggersticks, Ted explains. You can't buy one, and no true jiggerman would use store-bought gear anyway, even if it were available, which, of course, would discourage anyone from trying to mass-produce it in the first place. There aren't more than a hundred true jiggermen left, Ted estimates. Most are old men on fixed incomes and they admit acolytes like me into their circle reluctantly. It's not a burgeoning market. So all jiggering equipment except line and reel is handmade. It's a point of pride among jiggermen.

The jiggerstick is barely three feet long from tip to butt. The handle is about a foot of hardwood, somewhat thinner than a broomstick. Taped to the handle is a tiny spinning reel loaded with four-pound monofilament. Two feet of thin fiberglass, with one extra-large taped-on guide plus a tip-top, stick out of the handle. "Buy a cheap spinning rod," Ted says, "cut off the tip, throw the rest away. You want solid fiberglass, not hollow. It's gotta be real sensitive for jiggering."

He knots his "jigger" directly to the end of the line ("never use a damn swivel"). Jiggers, too, are homemade, either from a silver or bronze willow-leaf spinner blade or a Swedish Pimple. The concave side is filled with solder so that the jigger serves as both sinker and flashy attractor. It's armed with a single hook—a No. 6, I estimate, and pinprick sharp.

Ted rummages among the inside pockets of his shapeless, bloodstained snowmobile suit, where his body's warmth keeps them wiggling, and comes out with a Styrofoam container of worms. He pinches off about an inch of worm which he threads onto the hook.

"Any bait works," he says. "Worms, salmon eggs, even that synthetic glop. Best of all is a perch eye. But first you gotta catch one."

He stands over the hole and free-spools his worm-tipped jigger down into it. When the line stops paying off his reel, he engages the bail, reels up one turn, gives it a couple of sharp jerks, settles his torso onto his hips, and gazes up at the sky. Wilson stands up, walks all the way around Ted, sits again, and whines.

Ted stands motionless, staring dreamily off into the distance. I suspect he has forgotten me, and if he didn't occasionally twitch his jigger, I'd believe he's forgotten he is jiggering. Suddenly he grunts, lifts his jiggerstick, and begins reeling. Then he mutters, "Ah, shoot."

His reel, set on a light drag, zizzes a bit before the toothy maw of a large pickerel appears in the hole. Ted hauls it out, unhooks it, and stuffs it headfirst back into the hole. "That ain't what we're after. Go ahead. You can try this hole."

Ted has loaned me one of his jiggersticks along with a jigger and my own container of worms. I rig up, lower my jigger, engage the bail of my reel, take a turn, give it a sharp jerk the way he did, and, as well as I can determine, I am jiggering. I stare at the line where it disappears through the slush in the hole. Then I try gazing up into the sky. I give my jiggerstick an occasional twitch.

By now Ted is jiggering in another hole fifty feet away. Wilson has headed for the pines, looking for nuthatches.

"Hit it!" Ted yells suddenly.

Reflexively, I lift my jiggerstick.

"Too late," he grumbles. "You gotta be *quick*."

I cannot imagine what he has seen from fifty feet away that I did not see for myself. I reel up my jigger. My inch of worm is gone. Well, my first bite. That, I think, is something.

By the time I rebait and lower my jigger, Ted has abandoned his hole and is cutting another. Wilson trots over to me, sniffs my boots, and wanders away. Snow has begun to spit from the sky. Ted was right. I wonder—

For some reason that I could never explain, for I am not aware of feeling or seeing anything, I suddenly jerk up my jiggerstick, and the spidery monofilament and the delicate fiberglass of my jiggerstick vibrate, transmitting to my fingers the pulse of a fish. I reel up. It's a yellow perch, about nine inches long.

This is what we have come here for. Jiggermen, Ted has emphasized, fish exclusively for yellow perch. To the jiggerman, at least, winter perch are the tastiest and prettiest and altogether most desirable fish in fresh water.

Well, I have caught thousands of yellow perch, every one of them by accident. I have targeted lowly species such as horned pout, bluegills, and crappies—not to mention certifiable gamefish such as trout and bass and lake trout—and sometimes schools of perch have filched my bait and spoiled my fishing, and I have cursed them.

Never once before today have I actually wanted to catch perch. Until this moment, I don't think I have ever paused to admire a yellow perch, either.

This one is as fat as a bass—a female beginning to swell with roe. Her pectoral fins are scarlet, as bright as fresh blood. Her black-barred flanks are golden, her belly platinum, and a faint lilac blush paints her chin. She looks tropical—too beautiful to be considered garish—lying on a patch of gray pond ice.

I shuck off my gloves, unhook her, break her neck, then look for Ted. I hope he's been watching and has witnessed my triumph. A hundred yards away through the sifting snow he is a blurry speck on the ice.

Wilson appears. He has a nose for fresh-caught perch, and he has come to lick mine. I rebait and drop the jigger back into my hole. I stare at the line, willing it to twitch and jerk. I am alert and ready.

Nothing happens. I am trying too hard, I figure. So I gaze up at the sky, the way Ted does. Maybe the perch bite better when they think you're not paying attention.

But, of course, I *am* paying attention, and when that doesn't work, I try to blank my mind. I notice that my toes have gone numb and my back has begun to ache. Jiggering, Ted has emphasized, is a stand-up sport. Sitting down is for tiltmen and for guys who merely jig. But it would feel good to sit down for a minute. I realize that my stomach is growling, that I'd love a mug of hot black coffee, that I have to pee—

There!

Another perch, this one an inch longer than the first, but skinnier—a male, I guess—is flopping on the ice.

I jigger for another ten minutes or so with no bites that I detect. I figure my hole has gone dry. So I slip a finger through the gills of my two trophies and go looking for Ted. His path is easy to follow. There's a slush-filled jiggerhole every fifty feet or so and beside most of them are a few spots of blood on the ice.

I find him around the other side of the island, standing there hipshot, staring at the sky, holding his jiggerstick at his hip. Wilson is lying on the ice beside him.

Scattered around them are at least a dozen yellow perch.

I drop my two among Ted's.

"Kinda slow," he grumbles. "Hell, I thought this snow. . ."

He lifts his jiggerstick, reels up another perch, snaps its neck, drops it to the ice. Wilson stands up, arches his back, licks the fish, lies down again.

"Looks like you've been doing okay," I offer.

He shrugs.

I kneel on the ice and pick up one of Ted's fish. She is at least a foot long, big-bellied and thick-shouldered. "This is a nice one."

He smiles—for the first time today, I believe. "Big old cow," he says. "Trophy perch. So you got a couple, huh?"

"Two, to be exact."

"Well, good. You're gettin' the hang of it, then."

"I don't know about that. I seem to catch 'em when I'm not paying attention."

"Zen," explains Ted. "It's like nymphing without a strike indicator." He has resumed his jiggering posture. His eyes have gone dreamy.

He catches another perch then jerks his chin at the chisel. "Hot hole," he says. "Spud yourself one right here beside me."

Ted's homemade chisel sends the chips flying. "With a good chisel and good technique, you should cut an inch of ice with each whack," Ted says. I know his chisel is good but my technique is crude, and by the time I've chopped through the five inches of hard ice, I'm sweating under my thermals.

And by the time I lower my jigger into my hole, Ted has abandoned his and wandered off to cut another—at least the twentieth he has cut so far. Jiggermen, I am learning, like all the good fishermen I know, are aggressive hunters. Holes go cold fast. You don't wait for yellow perch to come to you. There is nothing passive about jiggering. No time to sit down.

When I catch up to him again, he is standing over a new hole, munching a sandwich with one hand and sipping coffee with the other. His jiggerstick is wedged between his knees. Now and then he performs a knee bend to give it twitch. Jiggermen do not stop jiggering just to eat.

And so we jigger, move, spud new holes, and circle back to old ones. We try water so shallow that the jigger hits bottom almost instantly, and so deep that it seems to take a full minute for the line to spool off the reel before it stops.

From the deepwater holes, we haul trophy-sized crappies ("Some people think they're good to eat," sneers Ted. "They obviously never tried perch.") and big white perch, which we keep ("second only to yellows in the frypan"). From the shallow holes we catch pickerel and a few respectable largemouths, which go back headfirst. Ted curses every non-yellow perch. I secretly enjoy the mystery of not knowing what might come up through the ice but I keep it to myself and, like a dutiful apprentice jiggerman, I curse the bass and crappies.

Somewhere along the way the snow quits and sometime after that I notice that it's raining softly. Once, while gazing abstractedly at the black sky, I spot a bald eagle circling below the clouds. "Hey," I whisper to Ted, and I point. He nods. He's been watching it for some time.

I seem to enter a jiggerman's zone. I catch half a dozen fat yellow perch, one more or less right after the other. Nothing I am aware of feeling or seeing tells me a fish has taken but somehow I know, and when I lift my jiggerstick, it bends.

Zen, I guess.

Darkness comes early on a January afternoon, especially when the sky is heavy with clouds and a mix of snow and rain is falling. When Ted finally says, "Had enough?" I nod, and we gather up the perch that are strewn across the ice and stuff them into Ted's big mesh-cotton creel.

Those of us who consider ourselves sportsmen believe we have outgrown the need to measure the success of a day's fishing by the size and number of our catch. By that standard, jiggermen are emphatically not sportsmen, for Ted, I notice, is counting, and when we have stuffed the last perch into his creel, he says: "Fifty-three. Nine cows. Plus four big whities. Average day."

We trudge slowly back to our cars through the darkening woods and the knee-deep snow. Wilson follows at heel, and when a grouse explodes from under a hemlock, he lifts his head but does not bother giving chase. Wilson, like us, has spent eight intense hours jiggering. He's had enough sport for one day.

Part Three:

EXPOTITIONS

———◆———

"Oh! Piglet," said Pooh excitedly, "we're going
on an Expotition, all of us, with things to eat.
To discover something."
"To discover what?" said Piglet anxiously.
"Oh! just something."
A. A. MILNE, WINNIE THE POOH

. . . Spring Creek . . . might be a river crammed with
wild trout of great average size and great wariness,
a place where I had more interesting fishing chances
than I could imagine having anywhere else, but it
was also a place where I made some great friends
and learned more than I can tell.
NICK LYONS, SPRING CREEK

We haven't returned to that . . . wonderful river, and the
chances are good that we never will. The memories of
that trip still make my scalp prickle, but they are no
answer to my basic fishing need which, above all else, is
to fish as frequently as the mood strikes.
HAROLD F. BLAISDELL, THE PHILOSOPHICAL FISHERMAN

CHAPTER THIRTEEN

TREASURE HUNTING

M y favorite trout pond sits in the middle of some woods about an hour's drive north and west of my house. That's as much as I'm telling.

It has no name. It only covers two or three surface acres. To get to it you've got to follow an old tote road to a caved-in cellarhole, cross a meadow grown up to head-high evergreen mixed with gnarled old Baldwin apple trees, push through some briar and brush, cross several stone walls, climb one hill, then slog through half a mile of mucky swamp that breeds mosquitoes the size of hummingbirds. This is not fun. Lame-brained, actually, were it not for that pond.

Doc and I love that trek.

We've never seen tire tracks on the tote road or a cigarette butt or beer can or monofilament tangle on our little pond's brushy banks. No foot-worn path rings it. No outboard motor drowns the chirps of warblers and red-winged blackbirds or flushes the herons and ducks.

We like to believe we're the only ones who know of it, and that before the June morning when we pushed through the undergrowth and saw it for the first time, its glassy surface dimpled with trout rings, no man had ever wet a line in it. This is probably a delusion but it's a happy one, and we cling to it. It's our secret pond. We found it, and we guard its whereabouts as jealously as an old gold rusher.

We were fifty miles away when we discovered it one February evening ten years ago.

Doc had unrolled one of our topographic maps onto his kitchen table. "Lookit what I found, sonny," he said. He planted his forefinger on a tiny blue spot on his map, then used it to trace a single, dotted line. "Dirt road," he muttered. "The only road within miles." His finger stopped abruptly at a small black square. "Somebody may still live there. If so, we'll ask permission. Then," he continued, moving his finger across a greenish area, "we hike in. Cross this orchard and climb this hill. Gets steep. See how the contour lines are close together? Then we gotta negotiate this here swamp."

I leaned forward, getting into the spirit of it. "These feeder brooks," I said, tracing several hair-thin blue lines. "Spring-fed, I bet. Cold enough for trout. And look. This stream that empties the pond flows into this lake."

Doc grinned. "Exactly my point, young feller. I happen to know that lake's got trout in it."

So, as it turned out, did that pond.

Doc and I have discovered many of our most cherished fishing waters the way we found that trout pond—from the warmth of his kitchen in the deadest time of the winter. Fortified with our imaginations and a jelly jar of Rebel Yell, we spread his maps over the table, anchor the corners with our glasses, and put our heads together.

We study the blue legends. Here's a brook that angles away from the road. On the map we can read its meandering route through swamp and forest. Beaver dams, we surmise. We mark it on the map.

In April we'll launch Doc's little thirteen-foot Grumman, and armed with pushpole, paddle, loppers, fly rod, and keen anticipation, we'll push and haul our way upstream into its secrets.

And here's a pond that no road touches. It looks bassy on the map, judging by the marshy symbols around the cove on the western side. No concrete boat launch here, no cottages rimming its shores, no sandy swimming beach. A long, miserable trek in. Good. That's what we're looking for. Hell, something's got to live in it. Stupid, giant largemouths that have never seen a deerhair bass bug? Pickerel, surely.

Or maybe nothing but horned pout and chubs. It'll be fun to find out.

Sitting beside Doc's woodstove, our fancies blossom. We read stories from our maps. We populate the blue lines and blobs with giant uneducated fish. We strike gold.

How do we know what we'll find when we get there? Well, we don't. We create excellent fantasies but maps sometimes lie. Houses pop up like mushrooms, tote roads get paved. Crystal map ponds turn into mucky saucers in the woods and the icy mountain streams that tumble across the maps turn into dried-up rockbeds. That's okay. The treasure we hunt is rare and correspondingly precious. We expect plenty of wild goose chases. They spice the quest and make the rare discovery of a rich lode that much more rewarding.

But there are clues that reduce the risk. Doc and I follow up all rumors, especially those whispered by local old-timers and bribed from vagabond kids. State fish and wildlife departments keep records of ponds and streams that once made the stocking list but have since been abandoned. Any body of water connected, however remotely, to another known to hold a sought-for species is likely to contain that species. Ponds fed by mountain streams are good bets to harbor wild trout. Those whose outlets empty into bass lakes always hold bass.

Doc and I delude ourselves with the belief that the longer the hike and the rougher the trail, the more likely we are to uncover treasure. In fact, however, we've ferreted out some of our best spots within a two hours' drive and then a ten-minute walk from the city.

Doc and I began treasure hunting with topographic maps years before we discovered float tubes. His little lightweight aluminum canoe traveled hundreds of painful miles atop our shoulders. We still use the canoe to explore out-of-the-way brooks and streams in search of unspoiled trout fishing. We wear sneakers and pants we're prepared to get wet and muddy, because we know that we'll encounter places where we'll have to haul over blowdowns and around beaver dams and through riffles too shallow to float over. And we always bring the heavy-duty loppers that Doc uses to prune his fruit trees for hacking away the alder thickets that barricade the narrow parts of the stream. Generally Doc takes the stern, alternately paddling and push-poling, while I wield the loppers and the fly rod from the bow.

When we're hiking into one of those little nameless blue smudges on the map that spells pond, we wear our fishing vests, strap our float tubes onto our backs, loop our fins around our necks, and find the going easier than when we lug his canoe. Doc's thirteen-foot Grumman weighs thirty-eight pounds, about as light and portable as they come. But it goes awkwardly through thick brush and tends to bump into things and wedge itself between trees. My inflated float tube, by contrast, weighs barely ten pounds. Shouldering a tube leaves both hands free, one to fend off brush and slap at mosquitoes, and the other to carry my broken-down fly rod.

"Journey over all the universe in a map," advised Cervantes, "without the expense and fatigue of traveling, without suffering the inconveniences of heat, cold, hunger, and thirst." These are the romantic winter journeys that Doc and I make from his woodstove-warmed kitchen as we translate the magical tales told in our topographic maps. Come spring, we test those tales against reality. Wild goose chase or treasure trove—neither really disappoints us. Half the fun is getting there.

CHAPTER FOURTEEN

K.O.D.

A few years ago my fishing buddies went bonefishing at Dead Man's Cay in the Bahamas. They went without me. Never mind why I didn't go. As it turned out, my priorities were severely screwed up and my so-called friends wouldn't let me forget it. When they got back, they tortured me with photos and stories— endless miles of unspoiled flats, a solid week of warm sunny days and gentle breezes, thousands of happy tailing bones ranging up to six or seven pounds that ate anything that dropped onto the sand in front of them.

They wanted to go back. No way they'd leave me behind this time.

Early March. Back in New England, our wives were bracing for what the wizards of weather were calling The Storm of the Century, and so what if the century was only a couple of years old.

Meanwhile, on a hard-bottomed, mangrove-rimmed flat, Jerry, our guide, and Andy and I were creeping along in ankle-deep, seventy-eight-degree water. Jerry stuck close to my left shoulder. He had shrewdly sized us up and decided that Andy could manage on his own. I'd spent our first morning not seeing what Jerry and Andy were seeing.

Then: "Bones. Twelve o'clock."

Jerry pointed and I looked, but my bonefish eyes were still somewhere back in Belize where I'd left them a few years ago. "I don't see 'em," I said.

"Coming *at* you, man. Forty feet. Two of 'em. No. Three. They're turning left. Ten o'clock, now. Oh, beeg bones. See 'em?"

"*No,* dammit."

Spotting bonefish is the whole point of fishing for them. But I'd forgotten what I was supposed to be looking for. Shadows and ripples and turtlegrass and the high shimmering Bahamian sun created a thousand bonefish out there at ten o'clock.

Screw it. I made a cast. Was that forty feet? Was that ten o'clock?

"Queek. Thirty feet. Eight-thirty now. Comin' fast. Cast again."

I did.

"Yeah, good shot. He turned. He's on it, man. Streep. Slow. Stop. Okay, now streep. . . ."

I held my breath. Beside me, so did Jerry.

Then he let it out. "Looked at it. Didn't want it. Spooky ol' bones. Cold front comin', that's why. Bonefish, man, they can feel it."

A few minutes and forty yards later, again Jerry said, "We got bones." I thought I detected a note of resignation in his voice.

He pointed, and this time, *mirabile dictu,* I saw them, shadowy shapes ghosting toward us, and I couldn't understand why I hadn't been seeing them all day. It was a little patrol, eight or ten reconnoitering bonefish, at two o'clock.

"Got 'em," I said.

I dropped my fly five or six feet in front of them, let it sink, gave it a twitch, stopped, stripped again . . . and I saw one of the shadows turn, then felt the tug. I stripped, came up on him, lifted my rod, and he was off on that first, unforgettable bonefish sprint, my first of the day, my first in several years, a sizzling, panicky dash for deep water. I held my rod high and watched the line zing through my guides.

Oh, yeah.

Then my rod went limp.

Jerry laughed, then began sloshing across the flat where my fly line, now disconnected from my backing, was slithering away. One more in a lifetime of memorable knots.

When I caught up to Jerry, he was holding my line and grinning. "You still got your fish," he said. "He stopped running when he stopped feeling the pressure."

Jerry handed me the line and I hauled it in hand-over-hand and landed, if that's the word for it, a three-pound bonefish.

Off to my left, Andy was chortling and snapping pictures. "Behold the famous angling writer," he said.

An hour later, abruptly, we lost our sunlight. "The lights went out," observed Jerry. "Here comes the front. Look."

From the west, an immense cloudbank was sweeping across the sky toward us like a big black blanket being pulled over our heads.

"Me," said Jerry, "I'm going for the boat."

"It's gonna pour," I said.

"Rain's okay, man." He made exploding motions with his hands. "Don't like that lightning."

By the time Jerry returned with the boat, the rain was coming in torrents and thunder was crashing and the temperature had dropped about ten degrees. It was, he said, the first rain they'd had in a couple of months.

It passed over in less than an hour. In its wake came a sharp westerly wind and a brittle sun. We huddled in our windbreakers and shivered.

"Not good, man," said Jerry prophetically.

I am known among my fishing companions as Ol' K.O.D. The Kiss of Death. Take a trip with me and something will go seriously wrong. If you believe my friends, in 1996 I singlehandedly flooded the Yellowstone River over its banks and destroyed our beloved Paradise Valley spring creeks. It was I who summoned a blizzard upon the Bow River, a torrential rainstorm upon the Beaverkill, and a week of unseasonable gale-force winds—always the winds—on both of our trips to Belize.

That night at the poker table when they started in on me, I reminded them of what was happening back home. We'd all talked to our wives. They were buried under two feet of wet snow and it was still coming down. Predictions called for another day of it. They'd declared a state of emergency in Massachusetts.

"And here we are, boys," I said. "Playing poker on a screened porch, eating Bahamian bananas, sipping margaritas, wearing shorts and T-shirts. How bad is this?"

"Quite bad, actually," said Andy.

"Sammy says it's gonna drive the bones off the flats," said Elliot. "He says they've never had a cold front come through this late in the season." He pointed his finger at me. "He did it again. The ol' Kiss of Death. It took him just one day to wreck the fishing."

I suggested that we should all take a few minutes to feel guilty about leaving our families to contend with New England's Storm of the Century, but they weren't buying it.

That cold front dropped the water temperature on the flats a critical few degrees, and for a couple of days the bonefish were hard to find and harder to fool.

The barracudas and sharks, on the other hand, which typically express baleful indifference to a streamer dragged past their noses, seemed to have been activated by the cooler water. Rig up a wire leader and throw a long skinny fly—preferably something chartreuse—toward a 'cuda and strip as fast as you can. If he so much as twitches, you've got his interest. Cast again. Strip. Faster!

You've got to drop a big, colorful (red and white is a good combination) streamer within a foot of a shark's snout. He's got poor eyesight so move it fast to catch his attention. If he turns and follows, slow it down.

We hooked several four-foot 'cudas and sixty-pound lemon sharks when the bonefishing was slow. We boated none of them for a variety of reasons that all amounted to excuses. I never did ask the guides what they'd do if they had to bring one aboard but I recalled how Hemingway shot himself in the leg with his .45 when he boated a shark. Enticing them to follow a fly, seeing the predatory ferocity of their take, feeling their brutal strength on the end of my line . . . that was enough, thank you.

Fun. But they weren't bonefish.

Each day the wind abated by degrees and shifted out of the west. The air and the water began to warm up, and toward the end of the week the bones started showing up on the flats. We intercepted squadrons of ten to twenty fish that we found patrolling the edges of the rocky outer islands, and on a few occasions we encountered battalions of close to a thousand milling around in knee-deep water. One morning Steve and I took turns plucking bonefish from a vast school while a dozen big lemon sharks circled our boat. Neither of us had any inclination to get out and wade.

Frank had us cut back to twenty-pound tippet and crank down our drags so we could horse the bones in before the sharks nailed them.

We didn't always manage it. I can still see the shark that loomed up behind a bonefish I was about to land. He spread his jaws and showed me his teeth before he engulfed the panicky twenty-inch fish on the end of my line. Ah, Quint.

When I got home to New England, I found snow up to the windowsills. Vicki said the power had been out for three days, and the snowplow had knocked down our fence, and the roof had sprung a leak.

She pointed at me. "It's your fault, you know. Every time you go away something happens. You're the—"

"Honey," I said, "I know what I am."

CHAPTER FIFTEEN

A TALE OF TWO PONDS

U p until a couple years ago I had lived my entire life in the neighborhood of two Massachusetts ponds: Walden, which is the most famous pond in the world, and White, which is known only to us locals. When I was a boy nearly half a century ago, I pedaled my bike to both ponds to swim and to fish and to catch crawfish and frogs and generally to do the things that boys do at ponds. They offered good trout fishing then, and they still do. Trout are native to neither of them but they have been stocked for nearly a century and thrive in both. Double-digit browns are taken from both ponds every year.

In the early summer, trout don't begin feeding on the surface of the ponds where a fly fisherman might catch them on dry flies until dusk. At Walden, that is precisely when the loudspeaker announces closing time and calls in the fishermen. If you ignore the warning, your car is locked in the lot for the night.

I resent this regulation. I would prefer that the government did not govern me, even while I am grateful for the pond it preserves for me. And so I come to White Pond to fish in the evening instead of to Walden, because I want to be the one who decides when I will leave.

Had Henry David Thoreau built his cabin on the shores of White Pond (and he might have, so entranced was he with its beauty), the State Reservation would likely be located there, instead of at Walden, and everything would be different.

"That government is best," Thoreau famously wrote, "which governs not at all." And yet Walden still looks and smells and (except for the loudspeaker at dusk) sounds the way it did one hundred and fifty years ago because the government has insisted on governing it aggressively.

"Since the woodcutters, and the railroad, and I myself have profaned Walden," wrote Thoreau, "perhaps the most attractive, if not the most beautiful, of all our lakes, the gem of the woods, is White Pond;— a poor name from its commonness, whether derived from the remarkable purity of its waters or the color of its sands. In these as in other respects, however, it is a lesser twin of Walden. They are so much alike that you would say they must be connected under ground."

Like Walden, White Pond is a kettlehole, gouged from the earth by receding glaciers eons ago. It is spring-fed and bowl-shaped and surrounded by steep, sandy, pine-studded banks. Thoreau surveyed White and found it to contain "about forty-one acres," just two-thirds Walden's size. Like Walden, White Pond "has no island in it, nor any visible inlet or outlet." Only a few miles separate the two sibling ponds.

"White Pond and Walden are great crystals on the surface of the earth, Lakes of Light. . . . They are too pure to have a market value. . . . How much more beautiful than our lives, how much more transparent than our characters, are they!"

Today Walden is as crystalline and pure and muck-free and forest-rimmed as when Thoreau sojourned there—because the government owns it and the woods that surround it, and because its agencies forbid development or commerce on it or its shores. It is regulated with rangers on horseback, marked pathways, posted signs, admission fees, and loudspeakers.

White Pond, which was, when Thoreau knew it, unprofaned by railroads or woodcutters or solitary philosophers in one-room cabins, is today unprofaned by government regulations. A paved road leads to a popular public beach where matrons direct their toddlers to the water to pee. During the forty-odd years since I first pedaled my bike there, permissive zoning has spawned an architectural stew of cottages and houses that crowd helter-skelter against its shoreline. Concrete abutments and wooden boat docks jut randomly into the water. On a warm summer's evening, residents bring their folding chairs and boom boxes onto their little beaches and docks, where they drink beer and listen to rock music and laugh and flip cigarette butts into the water. If birds sing here, their music is drowned out by different drummers.

White Pond is governed not at all.

I like to fish locally. I *insist* on fishing locally. I love to plan adventures and to travel to distant places but I also need to be able to fish when the spirit moves me. I like to wake up, take my coffee onto the porch, and let the smell of the morning air inspire me to go fishing for an hour before I turn on my computer. And when afternoon shadows lengthen in my back yard and bullfrogs begin to grumble in my imagination, it's important to me that I can be fishing in ten minutes.

I don't always go. But I need to be able to go.

Now, towards sunset on this warm early-summer evening, I find the public beach at White Pond still mobbed. I feel conspicuous, carrying a fly rod instead of a picnic basket and wearing a fishing vest and waders instead of a bathing suit.

I know midges will hatch, and trout will come to the surface to eat them, when the sun leaves the water—just about the time the loudspeaker will blare over at Walden. So I've come to White.

Unlike Walden, no path circles the banks of White Pond for the convenience of walkers and Transcendentalists and fishermen. Here it's all private property to the waterline. I climb over a dock and then step around a middle-aged couple who are sitting in beach chairs with their feet in the water. They are wearing bathing suits and sipping from beer cans. The man is puffing a cigar.

"Excuse me," I mumble.

"You know you're trespassing," says the man mildly, as if he's said the same thing a dozen times already this evening.

"I'm sorry to bother you." I hurry past them.

"Good luck," calls the woman.

The easiest way to circle White Pond is to wade in the water where, technically, I will not be trespassing. It's noticeably warmer on my legs than Walden's, and the bottom is mucky, no longer cobbled with clean rocks as Walden's still is. The faint aroma of decay hovers over White Pond. Human habitation has closed in, and it no longer glitters like a crystal.

At the far end, halfway around from the public beach, I arrive at my destination—a shallow cove where woods, not buildings, rim the shore. Here I can fish peacefully for as long as I want. I wade out onto the bar that separates the cove from the main body of the pond. Here the water is cool around my legs.

A few fish are swirling in the shallows. Not trout, I know, but I cast to them anyway. I catch a couple of bluegills and one minia-ture largemouth bass. I lose myself in the rhythms of flycasting. The light is fading from the sky. Out toward the middle a lone trout swirls—not close enough to reach, but I cast in its direction anyway. It's probably cruising, and if it cruises in my direction . . .

A sudden splash directly behind me, then another, then laughter and loud adolescent voices. I glance back. A boy and a girl in bathing suits are pushing at each other, wrestling, up to their knees in the water, laughing. The boy throws a rock—not exactly at me but out into the pond where I am casting. The girl tries to throw one in the same direction. It falls short of his. The boy grabs her arm and pulls her underwater. They come up giggling and grappling at each other.

"Nature," wrote Thoreau, "has no human inhabitant who appreciates her. The birds with their plumage and their notes are in harmony with the flowers, but what youth or maiden conspires with the wild luxuriant beauty of Nature?"

Not, certainly, this youth or this maiden. Thoreau is right: Nature "flourishes most alone, far from the towns where they reside."

"Hey," calls the boy. "You catch anything?"

"Not yet," I answer.

"Come on," says the girl. "We're scaring his fish."

The kids slosh to shore and disappear.

Now the surface of the pond lies as flat and dark as a sheet of carbon paper. I can still hear the faint thump of music from the other end of the pond but it is muffled by the mist rising off the water.

A bat flaps overhead. Behind me, a frog burps. Some swallows swoop over the water. Their wingtips tick the water, leaving rings like rising trout.

And other rings appear—a few, at first, way out beyond casting range. The swirls catch the light of the setting sun, and they spread, moving closer, and now, quite suddenly, the pond is pockmarked with the rings of rising trout.

I wade out until the water is over my hips, spot a rise, cover it. I let my little Griffith's Gnat sit motionless. Another rise, off to the right. Then another. I resist the urge to lift and cast again. I wait. I give it a tiny twitch. Wait, wait . . . A swirl. I lift my rod. It bends, and I feel the urgent life pulsing through my line to my fingers.

And now I am truly alone on White Pond, this Lake of Light, this gem of the woods.

CHAPTER SIXTEEN

ALASKA ON OUR OWN

"I 'll pick you up in a week," said Dave Klosterman, and he jabbed his finger at an X on a crude hand-drawn map. "Here. Three o'clock. Don't be late. I won't wait for you." He shook hands with all of us. "Good luck, boys," he said, and somehow it sounded ominous, as if he expected us actually to need luck. Then he climbed back into the plane, taxied down the river, and lifted off. The DeHavilland Beaver wagged its wings, and the six of us stood on the riverbank shading our eyes as it disappeared behind the treeline, heading back to Anchorage.

The drone of the plane's engine faded and died, and we were left with the quiet murmur of the river and the sough of the breeze in the evergreens. I suspect my partners and I were all thinking the same thing: Here we are, in the middle of the Alaskan wilderness, one hundred and fifty miles from the nearest road or telephone, and what happens if one of us gets a hook in the eye or breaks a leg or has a heart attack? What if we dump all our food into the river? What if we lose a raft? What about bears?

I know that scenes from *Deliverance* were playing in my head.

But we had rafts to pump, gear to lash down, and several miles of tricky rapids to negotiate before we arrived at our first campsite. It looked like rain, and the mosquitoes that were swarming over the narrow sandbar reminded us that we didn't have the luxury of idly standing around and pondering our fate. We had work to do.

Besides, this was exactly what we had come here for.

Bill Rohrbacher had called me from his home in Oregon a year earlier. "We're going to Alaska, man," he boomed.

"Oh, good," I said. "And you're paying, right?"

"King salmon," he continued. "Thirty, forty pounders. Brutes on a fly rod. You think tarpon can pull and jump, man."

"I guess you didn't hear me," I said.

"What, money? You worried about money?"

"Who isn't?"

"How's a hundred bucks a day sound?"

"It sounds like you're at the bottom of your rum jug, Bubba. Just paying a guide—"

"No guide," he interrupted.

"How're we gonna do Alaska without a guide? Anyway, the lodging—"

"No lodge, either."

"Oh, sure. No guide, no lodge. Great."

"It *is* great. It's do-it-yourself. Row our own rafts. Camp on the riverbank. Cook for ourselves. Fish all night. Shit in the woods. Slap mosquitoes. A true wilderness experience. You with me?"

"Since you put it that way, how can I refuse?"

Bill explained how it worked. All we needed to bring was fishing equipment, sleeping bag, and clothing. We'd buy a week's worth of food in Anchorage. Klosterman's outfit, Alaska Bush Carrier, provided all the rafting and camping gear. They'd fly us into the river and pick us up somewhere downstream seven days later.

Not counting airfare to Anchorage, it actually worked out to $88 per person per day.

It never gets dark in Alaska in the first week of July, and the chinooks were running up the Tal. They rested in holes and runs that we learned to identify, and for the first couple of days the six of us fished hard and slept little. They were, as Bill had promised, powerful gear-busting fish. We broke off or otherwise failed to land three or four for every one we landed. Some of them leapt like their Atlantic cousins. Some bulldogged against the heavy river currents, using boulders and snags to their advantage. Some took off downstream, determined, it seemed, to return to the sea whence they had come.

We used ten-weight fly rods, minimum stick to throw three-hundred-grain sinktip lines and to wrestle those mighty fish. Sturdy disc-drag reels with two hundred yards of backing. Cast across the current, mend upstream, let the fly sink and drift past the noses of those orange blurs resting their bellies beneath the heavy flow. Now and then, whether from irritation or predatory habit, one of them opened his mouth and sucked it in.

Most of those we landed were in the thirty-pound range. Andy tailed a couple that exceeded forty. We lost a few that looked even bigger.

Once we had all caught a few salmon, we relaxed and adjusted to the no-deadline tempo of our trip. While some of us fished, others cooked or napped. When you can still see well enough to tie on a fly at two in the morning, it ceases to matter when you sleep, and any meal could have been breakfast. We ate a lot of ham and eggs and fried potatoes and drank coffee continuously.

We pitched our tents on sandbars beside holding runs and moved to new campsites every two or three days, working our leisurely way downriver toward our rendezvous at the X on Klosterman's map.

Some days it rained, and we were grateful for high-quality rain gear and thermal underwear and sturdy neoprene waders. Some days the sun blazed out of a clear summer sky, and we fished in T-shirts with our waders rolled down to our waists.

Generally there was enough breeze to keep the river and the campsite relatively mosquito-free. For our necessary daily excursions into the bushes, though, Muskol was as important as toilet paper.

"Bring lots of flies," Bill had advised. "Ten dozen isn't too many. You'll bust off a lot of fish, and the river's full of rocks. Anyway, you never know what color or pattern or size or shape will turn them on." I tied generic patterns that featured marabou and bunny strips and soft hackles and Krystal Flash. Pink and chartreuse, red and purple, blue and orange, yellow and black, on No. 2 and 1/0 salmon hooks, some with lead eyes, some unweighted. Nothing fancy.

As it turned out, good old black woolly buggers worked as well as anything.

The Talachulitna, more or less due west of Anchorage, joins the Skwentna, then the Yentna and the Susitna before it empties into Cook Inlet. The Tal alternates long flat runs, boulder-strewn rapids, and deep cuts between steep canyon walls. We had a few genuine white-water adventures, and in a couple of places we had to line our rafts through rapids too risky to float. In the runs we stopped to fish, the Tal was comfortable to wade, and a sixty-foot cast covered the water.

King salmon begin entering these Alaskan rivers in June. The cohos start to appear in August. There are always rainbows and grayling, although the trout fishing is best after the salmon have begun spawning. The Tal was once a superior rainbow river but heavy fishing took its toll. Now it's catch-and-release for trout, and they're coming back. We accidentally caught several over twenty inches on salmon flies, and we had some evening fun casting humpies and royal Wulffs on trout rods, just for the feathery feel of the four-weight after slinging heavy sink-tips all day.

Nobody stuck a hook in his eye or broke a bone or got sick. We played poker and took turns cooking and shat in the woods and grew beards. Eagles soared overhead continually, and one midnight a sow grizzly came to the river for a bath. We caught king salmon until our arms ached.

We almost lost one of the rafts (the one carrying most of the food and half of the tents) as we lined it through some boulders in the first hour of the first day. As we scrambled to rescue it, I think we all realized that we really were on our own in this wilderness with only each other to rely on. Klosterman would meet us at his X in a week, and that was that. It was sobering—but exhilarating, too. This, we agreed, was what an Alaskan experience should be.

It was worth a helluva lot more than $88 a day.

Part Four:

BESIDES TROUT

———⋙⋘———

It seems not to have taken American fly fishers long to recognize the sporting possibilities of the nonsalmonids. By the 1840s, fly fishers were regularly taking the various basses and sunfishes, as well as pike and other occasionals, on flies in many parts of this country.
PAUL SCHULLERY, *AMERICAN FLY FISHING*

I want a fish that is fastidious and finicky, wily and skitterish, hard to lure, game when hooked. . . . I am hard to please; but there is, among all the many kinds of fish that swim, one, just one, that fulfills all my many requirements.
WILLIAM HUMPHREY, *MY MOBY DICK*

Trout are quite unaware of their exalted status. All the romance of trout fishing exists in the mind of the angler and is in no way shared by the fish.
HAROLD F. BLAISDELL, *THE PHILOSOPHICAL FISHERMAN*

CHAPTER SEVENTEEN

——⟫◦⟪——

LIFE LIST

Toward the end of June, Marshall Dickman and I found ourselves wandering around the Finger Lakes region of upper
New York State, where the rolling pastoral landscape is wrin-
kled like the back of an old farmer's neck and cold water tumbles
through every crease on its way to one of the ten skinny lakes. We were
chasing down rumors that big trout and salmon lived in those little tribs.

Alas, it had been a hot dry spring, and then the week before our
arrival some thunderstorms had blasted through, so that we found
the streams running low and warm and muddy, an unusual—and
unusually bad—combination.

Our friend Ron Avery, who guides trout fishermen and turkey
hunters all over the area, had volunteered to show us some of his
favorite places. But after a couple days of so-so fishing, we were
forced to conclude that the terrible water conditions had driven the
trout down into the lakes.

We were reconnoitering over plates of corned beef hash and home fries and over-easy eggs and mugs of diner coffee. Ron was apologizing for his streams, and Marshall and I were apologizing for our lack of angling skill. It was a dreary conversation.

Then Ron said, "You guys want to try for some Kamloops? I know a secret spot."

"Absolutely," I said instantly.

Marshall arched one eyebrow at me and gave a little shrug. I guessed he was thinking what I was thinking: What the hell is a Kamloops, exactly?

"It's a kind of rainbow," said Ron, who's pretty good at reading body language. "Native to some remote mountain lake in Idaho. They grow big and strong. A subspecies, I guess."

"I knew that," said Marshall.

"I should hope so," I said.

Actually, it didn't matter what exactly a Kamloops was. I'd never in my life caught one on a fly and that made it a most desirable fish.

My fly-fishing partner Jon Kolb is also a dedicated bird watcher. Last summer we were in the middle of a delicious pale morning dun hatch on a Montana spring creek when I saw him suddenly stop casting. He cocked his head, then reeled in, slogged to the bank, and took out his binoculars. When I accused him of dereliction of duty, he said he thought he'd heard the call of some rare warbler he'd never seen before and wanted to confirm its identity.

Unlike a lot of devout birders, Jon doesn't keep a written "life list" of the species he's seen. But he has a mental list. Mention a bird to him and he can instantly tell you whether he's ever seen one, and for the rare ones, he can recall the date, location, and weather conditions. He's traveled to distant places for the chance to spot new species. He never goes anywhere without his bird book and his field glasses.

My friend Mike Fosburg does not fish or watch birds. He climbs mountains. His goal is to scale the tallest mountain in each of the fifty states. So far he's conquered twenty of them, from Maine to Nevada to Nebraska. He records them in a notebook. Just glancing at his list, he says, reminds him of the adventures he's had. Adding a new mountain to it gives him a sense of purpose and accomplishment.

I have my own life list. It enumerates all the species of fish, freshwater and salt, that I've caught on a fly in nearly six decades of fly fishing. (Here I pause to write them down, which I've never bothered to do before. The total is thirty-nine.) My list includes chubs, shiners, and suckers as well as tarpon, Atlantic salmon, and steelhead.

I don't count the fish I've nearly caught. I don't even want to talk about the permit that I fought to exhaustion (his and mine both) and brought alongside the boat before my knot pulled loose, and never mind the lemon shark that chomped through my leader or the muskellunge that swirled behind my Deceiver. They were memorable fish, for sure. But "almost" doesn't count on the honorable man's life list.

I observe three simple rules when considering a candidate for my personal life list:

1. I must catch the fish on a fly and a fly rod. The Moosehead lake trout that took my trolled Grey Ghost therefore counts. I put an asterisk beside the Salmon River steelhead I caught on an eleven-foot noodle rod, about an ounce of split shot, and an egg pattern, and I was uncomfortable about counting it until I caught one on my old 7-weight and an unweighted stonefly nymph.
2. I must actually be fishing for that species when I catch it. The flounder that somehow managed to eat the Clouser I was casting on the Monomoy flats for stripers did not

count. With my life list in mind, I immediately announced that I was thenceforth fishing for flounder but all I could catch for the rest of the day was a bunch of stripers.

3. It's my list, so I'm the one who decides whether a fish is "new" or not. I say a steelhead is different from a rainbow trout, and an Atlantic salmon is not a landlocked salmon, regardless of their scientific taxonomies. Likewise, I count subspecies as separate fish if I can identify them as such. Snake River and Yellowstone cutthroats, easily distinguished, are two separate fish on my list. On the other hand, I've probably caught more than one strain of brown trout but since I can't tell them apart, they count as just one fish on my list.

Until a few minutes ago, I had never written down my life list or counted the number of fish on it. But if you mentioned a species to me, like Jon Kolb with his birds, I could instantly tell you if I'd ever caught one, and, for the rare or difficult ones, where and when I caught my first, and biggest, and most recent one.

Mike Fosburg theorizes that list-keeping is a growing-old thing. It's less about remembering what you've done and more about continuing to have goals. He says he climbs different mountains because it gives him an excuse to visit new places and to seek new challenges. Life, he says, is all about accumulating experiences, and every new mountain is a new experience for him. Keeping a list of the mountains he's climbed—the short gentle ones equally with the tall dangerous ones—and adding to it regularly is his way of assuring himself that he hasn't stopped living.

That's pretty much how I feel about fish.

Those close calls with permit and sharks still haunt me. I traveled far for the chance to catch them, and I failed. Don't get me wrong. I had a lot of fun casting to them, seeing them take my fly, and feeling them rip line off my reel. I suppose if I were a better man, that should've been enough.

I can't help it. I really wanted to add them to my list.

Ron Avery's secret Kamloops spot turned out to be a one-acre farm pond. The fields were mowed right down to the water's edge, and a wooden casting platform extended out over the water. There was a picnic table and a charcoal grill, an outhouse and a tool shed. Not what you'd call a remote mountain lake.

But a Kamloops was a Kamloops, and I'd never caught one. Ron swore this little pond was full of them.

So I walked out to the end of the platform, tied on a black woolly bugger, and cast it halfway across the pond. Let it sink to the top of the sunken weedbed. Twitched it back.

Nothing.

Ron and Marshall were casting, too. I saw a few flashes down among the weeds, and once or twice I thought those flashes might've been behind my fly. We all kept changing flies but after fifteen or twenty minutes, no rods had bent.

Ron went to the shed, picked up a tin can, and came out on the casting platform with me. "Watch this," he said, and he reached into the can and tossed a handful of pellets into the water. Abruptly the surface began to boil with feeding trout. Now I could see that these Kamloops were nice fish. Seventeen or eighteen inches, it looked like.

I cast my bugger out among those frenzied rainbows, gave it a twitch, and held on.

Nothing.

After a few minutes, the feeding frenzy subsided.

Okay, I thought. Good. They are trout. They feed selectively. Here on this pond, yellowish pellets the size of double-ought buckshot are hatching. Match the hatch.

I tied on a plump size 18 gold-ribbed hare's ear.

"Give 'em more pellets," I told Ron.

He did, and again the surface churned with hungry trout.

I flicked out the little nymph and let it sink. I watched my leader, and when it twitched, I tightened, and my rod bent in half. The fish slashed back and forth across the little pond, and when I finally cradled him in my hand, I thought he might've looked a little different from other rainbows I'd caught.

I slipped him back into the water, reeled up, and put down my rod. Mission accomplished. I'd added a Kamloops to my life list.

Now it was time to think about my first fly-rod carp.

CHAPTER EIGHTEEN

THE SNIPER

My first close encounter with a pickerel nearly caused me to give up fishing forever. I was eight or nine years old at the time. It was one of those lazy afternoons of a boy's endless summer, and I was, as usual, sitting on the grassy bank of my local millpond dangling a worm under a wine-cork bobber. I had shucked off my sneakers and socks so that I could wiggle my toes in the warmish water while I studied the neon dragonflies and damselflies that perched on my old glass fly rod and listened to the bullfrogs that grumped in the weeds and waited for a bluegill or a perch to come along and set my cork a-quivering.

The fish seemed to materialize in the water at my feet. He wasn't there, and then, suddenly, he was. He lay there staring at me, suspended motionless just beneath the surface, almost perfectly camouflaged in the weedy green water, and I was certain that his baleful eyes were focused on my tender white toes. They were the eyes of a predator, malevolent and single-minded and purposeful and altogether fearless.

He must have been two feet long, and he seemed even bigger. He had long powerful jaws and a mouthful of teeth and a sleek muscular body. He was a primitive killing machine, perfectly designed to strike suddenly and swiftly and to slice off a boy's toes.

I scrambled away from the bank and hastily yanked my bobber and bait out of the water. The thought of that vicious creature on the end of my line was almost as scary as the prospect of losing a toe.

I have never quite recovered from my first up-close and personal glimpse of a big pickerel. I've caught hundreds of them in the forty-odd years since that summer afternoon at the millpond. But they still scare me.

Thoreau, that noted dissenter, said of chain pickerel: "They possess a quite dazzling and transcendent beauty. . . . They are not green like the pines, nor grey like the stones, nor blue like the sky; but they have, to my eyes, if possible, yet rarer colors, like flowers and precious stones, as if they were the pearls, the animalised nuclei of crystals of the Walden waters."

Well, *chacun á son goût.* Most fishermen of my acquaintance consider the chain pickerel downright ugly, and a nuisance to boot.

They can be a nuisance when little ones slash at deerhair bass bugs and bluegill-sized poppers. Small pickerel (a foot or less) have teeth like scalpels which can slice through a leader tippet so cleanly that when you lift your rod to set the hook, you feel nothing.

But even when that happens, it's almost worth it. Unlike most predatory fish, which actively search for victims, pickerel are snipers. They hide in motionless, perfectly camouflaged ambush along the edges of weedbeds or fallen timber, waiting to strike anything living and edible—or anything that *looks* living and edible—that comes along.

When a hungry pickerel spies a victim, he slips from his hideout to pursue. Slowly at first, he takes its measure. If it's your fly he's after, you might spot a wake ten feet or so behind it. If a pickerel had a more prominent dorsal fin, you'd suspect a shark.

The attack comes suddenly and with lightning speed. The wake accelerates, and then your bug disappears in a swirling heart-stopping implosion of water.

The pickerel is a gamy fighter—pound for pound, stronger and swifter than a largemouth bass. He leaps, bulldogs, and runs, and when you think you've got him beat, the sight of your boat or net inspires him to fight some more. But as feisty as pickerel are, that strike is the best part.

There are plenty of effective ways to catch large pickerel. These are the traditional New England bait-casting methods: Suspend a lively three-inch shiner under a bobber and drop it along the edge of a weedbed; or, impale a strip of pork rind on the single weedless hook of a Johnson spoon and slither it through a growth of lily pads; or, cast a big Dardevle to fallen timber and other shoreline structure.

Old-timers caught their pickerel by "skittering" a six-inch strip of perch- or pickerel-belly across the top of a weedbed with a twelve-foot cane pole and a fixed length of strong line.

All those traditional methods still work, and all of them, in their own way, are fun. But pickerel make ideal fly-rod game fish. They prefer shallow water (six feet deep or less), and on a sunny day they often bask just under the surface. They always lurk around delicious fly-rod "targets." Probe alleys and potholes among lily pads. Work the edges where sunshine meets shade, where shallow water drops off, where one kind of cover rubs against another. Bankside brush, fallen trees, submerged weedbeds—anywhere pickerel can hide is where to cast for them.

Pickerel range across the entire eastern half of the United States and into southern Canada. They are the only native warmwater gamefish in the Northeast. They were here before largemouths and smallmouths, and they survived and prospered because they adapted to a wide range of water temperatures and because they foraged unselectively. They coexisted in big coldwater lakes with landlocked salmon and in glacial kettle ponds and beaver ponds with brook trout. But they fared equally well in shallow eutrophic ponds and sluggish rivers and sloughs and creeks.

The world record pickerel was a ten-pound, four-ounce monster taken in Quebec. The United States record was a nine-pound, four-ounce brute from Georgia. A four-pounder (about twenty-four inches) is a genuine big one, and a two-pounder is a worthy pickerel. Anything longer than two feet is a trophy.

Those who eat them claim they are delicious, and a variety of clever techniques have been devised to neutralize their pesky Y-shaped bones. Personally, I have no desire to kill a pickerel. They are useful fish that prey on whatever is most available and keep other populations in balance. Anyway, I'd rather have a big pickerel in the water where I can try to catch him again.

Yellow perch, where they exist, are probably the pickerel's favorite food but they eat all bite-sized fish (including other pickerel), crawfish, frogs, water snakes, small mammals and birds, dragonfly and damselfly and other big nymphs, and terrestrial insects. I still suspect they also eat the toes of small boys, when they're available.

Pickerel feed avidly year round. They are popular ice-fishing quarry, and for the fly fisherman, they offer fast action when nothing else does—when the ponds and creeks are rimmed with early ice and, later, immediately after the ice has gone out. Because they are sight-feeders, they hit best during daylight. Unlike many gamefish, pickerel are not deterred by bright sunlight. I've caught some of my biggest pickerel under a blazing midday August sun.

A big Mickey Finn streamer retrieved fast and jerky can't be beat, although in the weed-choked water that pickerel prefer, a fly tied on a keel-hook or rigged with some weedless device is almost mandatory.

In my opinion, though, the best way of all to catch pickerel—if you've got the heart for it—is right on the surface where you can see it happen. Pickerel can't resist long, slithery bass bugs that burble and gurgle when you give them a tug.

Color probably doesn't matter as much as motion. All-white and red-and-white are popular and effective. But as my father used to say, "For pickerel, any color is good as long as it's yellow," because yellow perch are important pickerel prey. So all of my pickerel bugs feature yellow.

A seven- or eight-weight rod with weight-forward (bass-bug taper) floating line makes a good outfit for surface-fishing for pickerel. Add a foot of hard thirty-pound shock tippet (Mason, for example) to an eight-foot leader tapered to 1X. The reel is the least important item of equipment, and backing is unnecessary. Pickerel fight hard but rarely make long runs.

It's sensible to carry a big landing net. Secure the fish for unhooking and release by gripping him with the mesh. If you find yourself tied to a pickerel with no net handy, grasp him firmly (but not roughly) behind the top of his head over his gill covers. This will immobilize him. Crimp down the barbs of all your pickerel flies, both to facilitate the fast release of the fish and to minimize any encounters with those serious teeth.

Whatever you do, don't let a pickerel loose in the bottom of your canoe, especially if you're barefoot. My old fear, I eventually learned, was well-founded. They *do* go for toes.

CHAPTER NINETEEN

EASTERN STEELHEAD

I was leery of the whole deal right from the beginning, and if Andy hadn't been so damned eager I'm sure I'd never have done it.

But there I was, up to my hips in the icy river, slipping and sliding on the slick rocks with feet that felt like blocks of ice. The water temperature was thirty-nine degrees—fifteen degrees warmer than the air. Snowflakes the size of dimes swirled so thick that I could barely make out Andy's shape fifty feet upstream. He looked like The Great Snowman.

Lake-effect snow, they called it. It muffled the gurgle of the river and fuzzed the dark evergreens that lined the banks, and despite the fact that snowmelt was trickling down the back of my neck and the guides on my rod kept icing up, it was kind of pretty.

The best thing about the whirling whiteout was that it hid from sight all the other anglers. Before the snow blew in, there were dozens of them spaced out every fifteen or twenty yards up and down the river. I assumed they were still there, and I liked not being able to see or hear them. It created the illusion of solitude, and even though I knew it was an illusion, I appreciated it.

And I was beginning to think that illusion had a lot to do with eastern steelhead fishing.

I was slinging an ounce of lead up into the currents, high-sticking it down through the slot, stripping, slipping, knocking ice out of my guides, slinging, sliding, high-sticking, again and again, with an aching shoulder and frozen fingers and no expectation whatsoever that I'd hook anything except bottom for the umpteenth time, mainly trying not to fall in, wondering what the hell I was doing there.

A few years earlier Andy had spent a week on one of those British Columbia steelhead rivers that Roderick Haig-Brown had written about so lovingly. In that entire week, Andy hooked and landed one steelhead. Nobody else in the lodge hooked anything. He was a hero.

That experience had hooked Andy on steelhead big time. It established his benchmark for successful steelhead fishing—one hookup per week. Whenever he talked about that fish, his eyes blazed, and the memory of it gave him infinite patience for slinging, high-sticking, stripping, and slinging again.

"Hey," I yelled to him. "Any strikes or anything?"

"Nope," he called cheerfully. "Not yet."

"Not *yet*? Ha."

"We gotta pay our dues," he said. "They're steelhead, man."

Steelhead? Really?

As far as I was concerned, steelhead were native rainbow trout that were born in storied rivers in the Pacific Northwest, spent two or three years in the ocean growing muscular and silvery, then followed their noses back to their natal rivers to spawn. Steelhead were big and wild and scarce and hard to catch. They were the West-Coast equivalent of Atlantic salmon—the ultimate quarry for the freshwater angler.

These so-called steelhead we were fishing for, on the other hand, were born in a hatchery, raised on pellets, and planted by the tens of thousands in this river. They migrated downstream not to an ocean . . . but to a lake. Granted, it was a big lake. A Great Lake. But a lake. When the spawning urge brought them back to this river I was standing in, their goal was to return to the hatchery a few miles upstream.

No doubt they were big and silvery and strong, and after a morning of slinging and stripping and slipping and sliding, I had no trouble believing they were hard to catch.

But you couldn't convince me they were wild. And if they weren't wild, as far as I was concerned, they weren't steelhead. Neither, for that matter, was I at all convinced that we were fly fishing for them. Our friend Fran Verdoliva, who was the local steelhead guru, had advised us to leave our fly-fishing gear at home. "Your stuff won't work here," he said. "You better use mine."

Fran's stuff started with what he called a "noodle rod." It was eleven feet long and had the spine of *al dente* vermicelli. The reel was packed with a level two-weight floating fly line and two hundred yards of backing. Knotted to the business end was a two-foot fluorescent butt section, then a ten-foot four-pound tippet, with a six-inch dropper festooned with split shot.

A size 10 pink glo-bug was the fly of choice. This river hosted autumn spawning runs of "Pacific" salmon—chinooks and cohos, products of the same hatchery—whose eggs the steelhead gorged on. Sometimes steelhead anglers tied into one of the salmon—or an Atlantic salmon (which had never swum in a real ocean, either) or a "sea-run" brown trout up from the lake.

We didn't fly-cast with the noodle-rod rig. We stripped off fifty feet of line, loaded the limber rod with the considerable weight of the split shots, and catapulted it out there. It was spin casting without a reel. We used the rod's length to guide the glo-bug through the slots and runs and hold the line off the water. Its extreme softness enabled us to feel the tickle of the weight bumping along the bottom, to detect the subtle take of a fish (a theoretical issue as far as I was concerned, and easily confused with hooking a boulder), and to protect the delicate tippet from the powerful runs and sudden surges of a ten- or fifteen-pound steelhead, should we actually hook one.

It was all pretty ingenious and nicely adapted to the challenges on this river, where the hemlocks that crowded both banks made backcasting impossible and the fish were so pounded by anglers that they scraped the bottom of the river with their bellies and demanded absolutely drag-free drifts.

So let's see: These fish were hatchery-raised rainbows that had never sniffed the ocean, and we weren't fly casting. I wasn't even convinced a glo-bug should be considered a fly.

Otherwise we were fly fishing for winter steelhead. The weather made it feel authentic, anyway. Winter comes early on the eastern shores of the Great Lakes.

Around noon the snow let up, the wind shifted, and the temperature dropped. Andy and I clomped through the snowy woods to our car, set the heater to full blast, and ate our sandwiches.

"So what do you think?" he said.

"I'll tell you when my brain thaws."

"Sometimes," he said, "steelhead don't bite."

"Sometimes they do?"

He smiled. He had the memory of it. It made all the difference.

I told him how I supposed I'd romanticized steelhead fishing, how this river, which was less than a six-hour drive from Boston, Manhattan, Philadelphia, and many other population centers of the Northeast, seemed way too populated and domesticated, how this

noodle-rod stuff blurred the boundary between fly fishing and spinning, and how these hatchery rainbows that had never tasted salt
water weren't the steelhead of my imagination.

"Just think of 'em as big trout," said Andy.

I nodded. That helped.

It spat snow intermittently throughout the afternoon. We fished
into twilight with no strikes and didn't walk out until the woods
were growing dark. Paying our dues.

We were back on the river at eight the next morning, slinging
and stripping, slipping and sliding, cocooned in another lake-effect
snowstorm. I lost my rig to the rocky bottom four or five times. That
was it for excitement.

The snow stopped around midday, the clouds lifted, and suddenly the sun was blazing out of a high blue sky.

"Oh-*kay!*" said Andy.

"Okay *what?*"

"A little sun, a little spike in the temperature. Just what the doctor ordered."

"I don't know about your doctor," I said. "Mine ordered psychi-
atric observation."

An hour or so later, high-sticking my rig through the same slot
I'd been fishing all morning, I hooked bottom again. Then the soft
tip of my noodle rod twitched, dipped, and then the fluorescent butt
section moved sideways, and when I lifted the rod, it arced down to
the butt and line began screaming off the reel.

"Hey!" I said.

"Fish on!" yelled Andy, and all the anglers around us reeled up
and backed out of the water.

The fish surged down the river. I stumbled along after her, holding my rod high. The other fishermen all had a word for me as I
slipped and slid past them. "Way to go." "Hang on." "Nice fish."
"What'd she eat?" "Don't fall in."

We landed her about a hundred yards downstream from where I hooked her. She was a broad-shouldered bullet-headed hen, silvery and muscular. A hair over thirty-two inches on Andy's tape.

After I revived her and she swam away, Andy shook my hand and grinned. "Now what do you think?"

"I think that was the biggest trout of my life," I said.

CHAPTER TWENTY

THE FISH OF 1,000 CASTS

I suspect my mother noticed that my voice was changing, nudged my father, and said, "You better have a talk with him."

The Facts of Life was an uncomfortable subject for Dad and I'm sure he would've preferred to avoid it entirely. He waited until we were in the car on the way to some trout river, and he skipped right over humans—and birds and bees, too—and started telling me the life history of the Atlantic salmon. He described the passion of the "spawning urge" and used words like "milt" and "roe," and then he paused and said, "Understand?"

I assured him that I did. I grew up in a neighborhood of older boys. And when I expressed more interest in the fishing than the biology, he was clearly relieved. His paternal obligation fulfilled, he told me salmon-fishing stories. Dad had fished for Atlantic salmon with Lee Wulff in Labrador and Newfoundland back in the glory days. He had a lot of stories and I sucked them up.

"You owe it to yourself," he said. "You've got to go salmon fishing some day."

The older I got, the more insistent he became. "Go, while you still can," he'd say.

I knew it wasn't the way Dad remembered it anymore. There weren't as many salmon as there had been fifty years ago when he fished for them. I knew that you did not go salmon fishing with any particular expectation. You could fish for a week without hooking an Atlantic salmon. I knew that Atlantics were called "the fish of a thousand casts" as a conservative measure of the investment required to hook one. You could never predict which of those casts would bring a strike or whether you might make two thousand casts before you earned the right to hook two fish.

I knew that on their single-minded spawning runs, salmon did not eat. But they sometimes struck at a fly for reasons that they did not divulge to us. Aggression, possibly, or territoriality, or irritability. Perhaps the feeding response was so imprinted in their brains that, like human potato-chip munchers, they sometimes ate automatically even when they weren't hungry.

I knew that Atlantic salmon could be caught on the fly rod, although mostly they could not be caught. They hunkered at the bottom of a pool while a thousand flies drifted over their noses, and then, inexplicably, they might rise to strike the one-thousand-and-first.

I knew that salmon fishermen argued over fly patterns—dark or bright, sparse or full, small or large, feather or hair. It was unclear if the salmon cared but fishermen surely did. Classic Atlantic salmon flies imitated nothing in particular. Instead they were elaborate and artful, on the theory, perhaps, that salmon might want to possess them out of admiration for their beauty or that such a worthy fish deserved an elegant fly.

The only secrets in Atlantic salmon fishing belonged to the salmon. The fishermen knew the pools where the fish were resting. They knew that their choice of fly was mostly whimsy. They began casting at the top of the pool, swung the fly through the current, took two steps, and repeated the cast until they arrived at the tail of the pool. Then they moved back to the top, waited for the other anglers to two-step along, switched to a different pattern, and did it again. And they did this all day, dawn to dark, through four or five pools each day, and they did it again the next day, and if they did it for a week they might catch several salmon. Or they might never get a strike.

I knew all these things, and, in spite of my father's stories, the idea of Atlantic salmon fishing did not truly excite me. I was, by temperament, a trout fisherman. Give me feeding fish, selective and spooky and smart. Make it a problem and assure me that it has a solution, however complex, and I would gladly make one thousand casts, although I'd rather spend my time scheming how to make one perfect cast.

This salmon fishing presented mysteries, not problems. It struck me as random rather than logical. It required faith and tenacity. I doubted I had the temperament for it. I didn't want to admit it but Atlantic salmon fishing sounded monotonous.

No. Boring.

But I also knew I had to go while it was still possible—in my lifetime and in the lifetime of the species. It wasn't that I owed it to myself. But I felt that I owed it to Dad.

Three fly-fishing fanatics. More than a century of combined fishing experience all over North America. Enough equipment among us to stock a small fly shop. There were few trout rivers the three of us hadn't fished together, and there were none of any significance that at least one of us hadn't tried. We'd caught permit and tarpon and bonefish in Belize and Mexico and the Bahamas and the Keys. We'd caught Pacific salmon in Alaska and giant brook trout in Labrador. We'd caught steelhead and shad, bass and pike, stripers and bluefish, crappies and carp.

But none of us had ever even tried to catch an Atlantic salmon.

We chose the Margaree River on Cape Breton Island, Nova Scotia. The Margaree was one of the few significant salmon rivers whose pools were open to the public and where a guide was not required. We could explore it and confront its mysteries for ourselves. We were attracted to the Margaree, too, because on this river fishermen were not allowed to kill the salmon they caught. Only grilse could be killed. This policy, perhaps, was responsible for the high percentage of large fish in the river.

The Margaree was small and accessible and especially beautiful in October, and we knew, although we didn't discuss it, that even if we caught no fish, we would be rewarded.

We left Boston at eight on a Friday night in early October. Andy, the only one of us with a regular job, sacked out in the back seat. Bill insisted on driving the whole way. My job was to stay awake and tell Bill stories so he'd stay awake.

We traveled eight hundred and fifty miles through the night and half of the day for our rendezvous with the salmon at the Margaree. The salmon had swum two thousand miles through the Atlantic Ocean to meet us there.

You never know with salmon. On our first run through our first pool of our first day on the Margaree, the old-fashioned featherwing wet fly that my father had tied fifty years earlier stopped halfway through its swing, and I saw the boil and felt the tug and the surge, and then the salmon leaped, bright silver in the morning sun against the copper of the streamside maples. When I cradled him in my hand, Bill guessed he weighed about twelve pounds.

We fished three other pools that day but had no more strikes.

The next day it rained. We fished hard. No strikes.

On the third day it snowed. Andy caught a grilse on a bushy dry fly on our last run through the last pool of the day.

On the fourth day ice formed in our guides. No strikes.

On the fifth day, Bill announced it was time to get serious. The fish were sulking on the bottom, he figured, and they needed to be stirred up. So he switched to a sink-tip line, a big flashy marabou streamer, and a nine-weight rod. "Steelhead tactics," he said. And he caught two salmon within half an hour of each other from the same pool.

Andy caught his salmon on his last cast in the last pool on our last day. It measured forty-two inches and weighed, we calculated, twenty-seven pounds.

Meanwhile, I made the rest of my one thousand casts and most of my second thousand, too, and never had another strike. I did not become bored. I remembered that tug and surge and that silvery arc over the river. It could, I now knew, happen again, any time. If not this year, maybe next. I already had an investment in another salmon.

CHAPTER TWENTY-ONE

SELECTIVE PERCH

Nantucket in late November. Stark, raw, desolate, bleak, wind-whipped, barren. A state-of-nature sort of place. A place such as Thomas Hobbes might have had in mind when he wrote that the life of man was "nasty, solitary, poor, brutish, and short."

The tourists and the seasonal residents had left around Labor Day. Now the beachside summer places were shut down and boarded up, and their empty eyes stared out on an angry gray ocean. Most of the in-town spots, the shops and boutiques and restaurants and cafés, were closed. You could buy the basics—gas, groceries, hardware, and a hot meal. But the island now belonged to a few hardy year-rounders.

My son Mike was one of them, and my Thanksgiving visit to the island was to be an overdue father-son reunion. I didn't even bring a fly rod. "Don't bother, Pop," he had said on the phone, and I knew he appreciated the fact that I was making one of my rare non–fly-fishing trips. Usually I don't go anywhere if I can't fish.

Mike had urged me to visit in the summer, when the stripers and blues were crashing bait off Great Point and Cisco Beach. He'd had some good fishing but for one reason or another things hadn't worked out. And now it was too late for that.

The truth was, I hadn't approved of this deserted-island thing he was doing. Nantucket was okay in the summer. There was money to be made off the tourists. But now he was stranded on this godforsaken place, a three-hour ferry ride from civilization, living in someone's basement, doing odd jobs, growing a beard, writing unpublishable stories.

Who the hell do you think you are? I wanted to say. Thoreau?

I had resisted the impulse to tell him how I felt. He hadn't consulted me and he was an adult now. It was his life to squander if he wanted to. At least that's what I'd been telling myself.

But still, it was good to see him, my son, now a man—even if he was an aimless, irresponsible one—after too many months apart, and we spent a day and a half walking the wind-swept beaches and driving through the countryside. We spotted deer and late-migrating birds and caught up on each other's lives, and I managed not to ask him if he had any plans.

After lunch my second day there—which happened to be Thanksgiving—he cocked his head, smiled at me, and said, "You'd really rather be fishing, wouldn't you?"

"That's okay," I said. "I've got to catch the ferry back tomorrow morning anyway. I've got a lot of work."

"I know how itchy you get," he said. "But there's nothing in the ocean."

I shrugged. "Don't worry about it."

"Well," he said, "maybe I got an idea."

He knew a little landlocked freshwater pond, he said. He'd heard it held some big pickerel. He had a couple of old fly rods and a box of streamers. We could try it if I wanted.

Of course I did.

The pond lay at the end of a winding pair of ruts in the middle of the island. It covered just three or four surface acres, almost a perfect oval tucked into a crease in the rolling brown late-autumn hills. It looked shallow and mud-bottomed and sterile, with no distinctive features. It was surrounded by wild rose tangles and scrubby gorse and sere marsh grass. It didn't look fishy to me.

We found a couple of pickerel-size Mickey Finn bucktails in Mike's streamer box. He headed clockwise along the shoreline and I cast my way in the opposite direction. The bowl of the pond sheltered us from the harsh sea wind, and it was warm and sunny and altogether pleasant. So what if we didn't catch anything? Fishing was never a waste of time.

After fifteen minutes we had fished our respective ways around to opposite sides of the pond. I'd had no strikes but I hadn't expected any. I figured Mike's pickerel rumor was false, or at least exaggerated.

Then he shouted, "Hey!"

"Hey what?"

"I had a strike."

"Yeah?"

"Well, more like a nip," he said. "Whoa! There's another one."

"You're supposed to catch 'em," I said.

Pickerel, I knew, did not "nip." They attacked. I guessed Mike's fly was ticking bottom and the rest was his imagination. He'd always had a powerful imagination.

Then I had a nip. The power of suggestion, I figured. Then came another nip, and when my streamer came into sight in the murky water, I saw a flash of yellow behind it.

And just about the time I figured it out, Mike yelled, "They're perch."

A six-inch yellow bucktail is the perfect pickerel fly. It closely imitates a yellow perch, which is important pickerel prey. But a big Mickey Finn isn't the fly of choice for yellow perch.

I reeled in and walked around the pond. Mike had the flies.

When I got there, he said, "I've tried every little bucktail and streamer in my box. Perch aren't supposed to be hard to fool."

"They're not," I said. "Are you fishing deep, twitching it back slow?"

He rolled his eyes.

I shrugged. "Sorry. Gimme some flies."

I grabbed half a dozen of the smallest things in his box, tied on a little white bucktail, and began casting. I let it sink, twitched it back slowly, had a couple nips but caught nothing.

Then I heard Mike grunt, and when I looked up his rod was bent. "Oh, yeah," he said. "Good one."

A minute later he held up a chunky foot-long yellow perch. A very good fish. And a pretty one, too, with its flashy lemon-yellow flanks, its coon-like black stripes, its crimson pectoral fins the color of fresh blood, its belligerent humped back. I'd caught a million yellow perch but I'd never really noticed how pretty they are.

"What'd he eat?" I asked.

"Little black leech. Sucked it right in. He pulled harder than a trout, I swear. Took me way too long to figure it out. These ponds are full of leeches. You gotta retrieve 'em real slow, pause for a count of five between twitches. They hit it when it's falling. You gotta watch where your leader enters the water for the little tug. Don't strike too hard. Just tighten on 'em."

"Yeah, good advice," I mumbled. "Hmmmmm. Selective perch. Imagine that. Got another one of those leech flies?"

"You've been giving me flies all my life," he said, dropping a black marabou leech into my hand. "This here's our last one. Don't lose it."

The inch-long leech fly, twitched slowly just off the bottom, did the job. I watched where my leader entered the water, tightened gently when I saw the little tug, and Mike and I caught yellow perch for the rest of the afternoon. They were cows, too—about ten inches to a foot long—and once we realized we were going to catch a mess of them, we kept a dozen.

As the sun began to sink behind the low Nantucket hills, something several dimensions bigger than a ten-inch yellow perch glommed onto my fly, and before it bit through my leader I saw that it was a pickerel. A two-footer, minimum. So much for rumors.

He took our last leech fly with him.

Mike insisted on doing the cooking. It took him just fifteen minutes to fillet that mess of perch. I didn't know he knew how to do that. I remembered when I had to stick worms on his hooks for him.

He deep-fried the fillets in batter and served them with a big green salad and cold beer down in his basement apartment, and those firm-fleshed November perch made the tastiest Thanksgiving dinner I've ever eaten.

While we were patting our bellies and sipping wine later that evening, Mike mentioned that Oh, by the way, he'd been accepted at graduate school. He was starting in January, and he'd be home for Christmas.

Part Five:

FLIES AND DESIGNS

———⊰◈⊱———

The trout really do take to designs better than patterns.
That is to say, they look at how a fly is behaving before
they consider its color. The concept of design makes sense
when you hear what the trout say. . . .
DATUS PROPER, *WHAT THE TROUT SAID*

I have always intended to tie a supply of scarlet dry
flies, or purple or orange . . . and fish with nothing else
for a spell. . . . I have a strong suspicion that these flies
would account for fully as many trout as would the
most painstaking selection from among standard patterns.
HAROLD F. BLAISDELL, *THE PHILOSOPHICAL FISHERMAN*

And with that he unloads . . . what looks like a dead
Barred Plymouth Rock chicken. . . . What it is is a
gigantic trout fly that Dog-Nose has tied out of a half-
dozen grizzly saddle-hackle patches and onto what
looks to be about a size 50/0 tuna hook.
CLIFF HAUPTMAN, *THE DOG-NOSE CHRONICLES*

CHAPTER TWENTY-TWO

THE ETERNAL DEBATE

It happened again last winter, this time in the form of an e-mail from my friend Skip Rood. "Just got home from a long and inconclusive—and at times acrimonious—discussion at the Boston Fly Casters," he wrote. "To settle it once and for all, I'm conducting a survey of my most trusted angling compatriots. I aim to compile the definitive list of the ten best trout flies. I hope you'll participate."

Several years ago, out of deference to a chronic cervical injury, I discarded my weighty fishing vest in favor of a small fanny pack. This required me to heed Thoreau's dictum to "simplify, simplify." No longer could I carry a dozen fly boxes, my lunch, my foul-weather gear, a pair of sneakers, emergency repair kits and streamside fly-tying kits and first-aid kits, tippets and leaders, spare reels and flashlights, fly floatant and insect repellent, split shot and strike indicators, and all the other junk that gave me a backache. My fanny pack holds two small fly boxes, a few spools of tippet, a couple of spare leaders, dry-fly floatant, bug dope, sunblock, a stale granola bar. Everything I need to get me through a day on the water . . . provided I have the right flies in with me.

Stocking those two fly boxes has forced me to debate the "best flies" question every day I go fishing.

I always resolve those debates by recognizing one important fact: It all depends.

I shot an e-mail back to Skip with these questions:

- Eastern or western trout? Moving or still water? Early or late season?
- When you say "flies," are you talking about specific patterns? Or do you mean designs? Do different sizes and colors count as separate flies?
- Why ten? Why not a dozen?
- And what the hell do you mean by "best"?

Skip's reply was succinct: "All-round trout flies. Anywhere anytime. Patterns. Ten because I said so, the ten patterns you'd have with you if that's all you were allowed. Rank 'em one to ten."

Okay, fair enough. Silly, but fair.

In the real world, the ten flies I'd want for a Montana spring creek in August would not be the ones I'd take to a Catskill freestoner in June or a Colorado tailwater in October, and none of those assortments would be what I'd choose for a Cape Cod kettle pond in April.

But if I were forced to pick just ten . . .

First, dry flies. I start with dries because I enjoy surface fishing the most. I go to places that promise dry-fly fishing at times when I expect trout to be rising, and I do not want to be without the flies I'll need to fool them. Since trout are generally more fussy about the surface imitations they'll take than subsurface flies, the choice of dry-fly patterns is most crucial.

Mayflies, caddis, stoneflies, terrestrials. Midges, for heaven's sake. Not even to mention spinners, emergers, cripples, floating nymphs. The well-prepared angler needs more than ten dry-fly patterns (each in several sizes) alone.

My father, in the spirit of experimentation, once spent two entire trout seasons using just one dry-fly pattern (his generic "Nearenuf") and claimed that he wasn't particularly handicapped. I know guys who fish with nothing but a parachute Adams. Others stick to a Royal Wulff. It strikes me as a pointless affectation, this stubborn refusal to try to match real insects, but these guys seem to catch their share of fish.

In fast-moving freestone, pocket-water streams, where hatches are sparse and bugs are scarce and selective trout go hungry, any old high-floating dry fly will work. But Skip said "anywhere, anytime."

Imitating mayflies alone . . . Eastern Light Cahills. Western Pale morning duns. Hendricksons. Tricos. Blue-winged olives. Drakes. *Callibaetis.* March browns. Sulfurs. Dozens of hatches that, at least sometimes, must be matched.

Just considering PMDs . . . at different times and on different waters, the trout seem to demand body colors ranging from pinkish to tan to olive to orange to yellow, and sizes from 14 to 20. Sometimes it seems to me they prefer quill bodies over dubbed, and parachute or hackle or comparadun or no-hackle designs.

Well, usually they're not that fussy. Get the size right and the color approximate, and I can take some fish.

I'll get by with two mayfly patterns, I think, provided I can carry them in a full range of sizes. One tan/yellowish and the other gray-ish. Light Cahill and Adams, then. In tiny sizes, they'll take care of my midge needs, too.

Elk-hair caddis makes three.

The Stimulator for stoneflies will also pass for hoppers. Four.

Foam beetle. My favorite "searching" pattern on slow, smooth water. Five.

Sparkle dun. My go-to emerger pattern. Number six.

Seven: Rusty spinner, for that crucial last stage of the hatch.

Seven surface patterns. I'm comfortable with that.

Which leaves three subsurface patterns. That's about the right proportion for me. I do about 70 percent of my trout fishing on the surface.

When nothing's cooking on the surface, and, of course, anytime it's apparent that trout are eating them, I tie on either a Pheasant Tail Nymph or a soft-hackle wet fly. One or the other will take care of just about all subsurface situations.

Nine patterns so far.

Number ten, when nothing else works: What anglers everywhere call "the good-old" Woolly Bugger. The Bugger catches fish anywhere, anytime, which is what earned it the right to be called "the good-old."

I submitted my list—in that order—to Skip, and a few weeks later he sent me the results of his survey:

1. Woolly Bugger
2. Parachute Adams
3. Elk-Hair Caddis
4. Pheasant Tail Nymph
5. Gold-Ribbed Hare's Ear
6. Foam Beetle
7. Stimulator
8. Muddler Minnow
9. Mickey Finn bucktail
10. Prince Nymph

Are you kidding me? What were these people thinking? Who needs a Prince Nymph? If you've got a Bugger, what do you want a Muddler or a bucktail for? What about all the tan/yellow mayflies you've got to imitate? And what're you going to do during a spinner fall? Or when they're eating emergers? Huh?

Before I could compose a message to Skip that adequately expressed my outrage, I got a phone call from my partner Marshall Dickman in the Hudson Valley. "Just got home from a meeting of The Angler's Club," he said. "Had a stimulating discussion, trying to agree on the four best trout flies. What do you think?"

Hmm. Four, I thought, was actually a more interesting problem than ten.

"Am I allowed to bring a pair of scissors with me?" I said.

"Well, sure. I guess so."

"These four flies. Can I carry them in different sizes?"

"Yes. That was stipulated."

"Okay," I said. "It's easy, then. Light Cahill, Adams, Elk-hair Caddis, Woolly Bugger. Nothing to debate."

"What about nymphs, emergers, and spinners?" he said. "What about stoneflies and terrestrials and scuds, for heaven's sake?"

"That's what the scissors are for," I said. "Cut, snip, slice. See?"

"Clever," said Marshall. "Though in the spirit of our debate, I'd call it cheating."

"The spirit of your debate," I said, "was to conduct a meaningless mid-winter debate, if I'm not mistaken."

Whenever I sit down at my fly-tying table to restock my fly boxes for the upcoming season, I gaze out my window at the snow-filled woods and recall the rivers and hatches and difficult trout of previous years, and I daydream about the places I hope to fish in the future. A winter afternoon of fly tying always promotes these reveries. If it didn't, I'd probably buy my flies.

The memories and daydreams help me to think about what flies to tie. Should I really devote a precious compartment in my fly box to gray drake spinners? I sure needed them that evening on the Henry's Fork.

What about those early black stoneflies? The trout never seem to eat them, but . . .

And then there was that *Hexagenia* hatch . . .

Whether you carry two fly boxes in your fanny pack or a dozen in your bulging vest, you cannot be prepared for everything. One way or the other, we all have to pick our ten—or four or twenty or one hundred—"best" flies.

It may be a debate with no answer. But it's not meaningless.

CHAPTER TWENTY-THREE

———≫·◆·≪———

THE UPSIDE-DOWN DUN

I devoted the better parts of several winter fly-tying seasons—squandered them, you might say—trying to design a dry fly that would consistently alight upside down on the water—that is, with the bend of the hook on top. This quest—okay, obsession—began several years back when I first read *The Trout and the Fly* by Brian Clarke and John Goddard, in which these two eminent British anglers make a powerful case for upside-down mayfly imitations.

For the spring-creek and stillwater trout fisherman, upside-downness is compelling: The bend of the hook penetrating clear, flat, slow-moving water looks decidedly unnatural and waves a red flag at squinty-eyed, selective trout—which happen to be the trout I most love to catch.

The law of gravity dictates that as a fly falls to the water, the hook bend will land first. To make the fly do what is unnatural—to design it so that it will violate gravity's law—calls on the same principle that prevents a hundred tons of flying metal from crashing to the ground: aerodynamics. If its wings, tail, and hackle work as rudders and stabilizers, a properly designed fly can, at least in theory, be made to flutter onto the water upside down.

Clarke's and Goddard's USD Paradun did exactly that. Even better, in photographs taken from underwater looking up to the surface—a trout's perspective—the USD Paradun, perched on its parachute hackles, looked exactly like the surrounding naturals.

I spent the better part of that first winter with their book open on my fly-tying desk. Their directions were absolutely unambiguous:

With the hook upside down in the vise, they mounted flared hackle-tip wings at the thorax. They then reclamped the hook in the conventional way and tied a stiff tail along the curve of the bend so that it pointed slightly downward. They tied in a monofilament loop on top of the shank, directly opposite the wings, as a post for the parachute hackle. They tied in the hackle feather, dubbed the body, wound the hackle, then pulled the loop tight with the tip of the hackle tucked in.

The authors wrote, with classic British understatement, ". . . these flies are not the easiest of patterns to tie, and . . . the dresser needs all the basic skills of the trade in order to produce a good finished article."

When I tried it, I had to question their definition of the word "basic." Tying a USD Paradun turned out to be frustrating and time-consuming. But I did eventually manage to produce a few that looked rather nice in the palm of my hand.

Alas, when I had the chance to cast them on the water, they showed no inclination whatsoever to look nice. Some of them simply sank. Others preferred gravity to aerodynamics and sogged there with their wings underwater. The trout laughed.

Back to the book: "With a little experience," Clark and Goddard wrote, "the length and width of the wings and density of the hackle can soon be judged, and the finished fly will then land right way up better than eight times out of ten."

I didn't know how much experience qualified as "a little," and perhaps I've got a bad attitude, but I've always felt that unless I can tie a fly easily and quickly and without too much aggravation, and unless I can look at the finished product and know that it will behave the way it's supposed to, it's simply not worth it.

I never did tie an eighty percent USD Paradun. After a while, I quit trying.

The next winter, still smarting from getting snubbed by too many fussy trout the previous season, I resumed my quest for an easy-to-tie, relatively foolproof dry-fly design that would keep the hook bend from penetrating the water. I consulted my friends and collected fly-tying books new and old . . . and got no help whatsoever. As near as I could tell, Clarke and Goddard had both the first and the last word on the subject of upside-down dry flies.

So I was on my own.

What follows is the chronological record of my efforts. Read this, if you want, as a cautionary tale.

1. The Backwards (BW) Parachute—I reasoned that if the wing and hackle stabilizers were mounted at the hook bend rather than toward the eye, their aerodynamics would overpower gravity more dependably, and the length and width of the wings, the density of the hackle, etc. would be less crucial. It also occurred to me that with the tail tied in at the hook's eye, the leader tippet would be neatly disguised as part of the tail, giving a backwards design one less red flag than any frontwards tie.

So I clamped a hook into my vise and, beginning at the eye, tied in the tail so that the fibers flared slightly downwards. Next I dubbed the body all the way back to the beginning of the bend. At this point I removed the hook from the vise, frowned at it for a minute, shrugged, and clamped it by the dubbed shank near the eye so that it stuck straight up from the jaws of my vise, with the bend of the hook on top. Then I tied a pair of hackle-tip wings directly onto either side of the hook bend and wound a hackle around the middle of the bend, under the wings and parallel with the shank.

Working all this material onto the bend of a size 14 dry-fly hook while trying to avoid fraying the thread on the hook point had me mumbling to myself. But the completed fly looked terrific, and when I cast it, I found that the proportions and specific locations of its components were not crucial to the way it landed on the water. It alit upside down more than eighty percent of the time. In this respect, I had actually bettered Clarke and Goddard. Best of all, when I drifted a BW Parachute over a trout that had been snubbing its nose at me, he gobbled it.

When I unhooked the fish, however, I found that his tiny teeth had destroyed the wings and hackle, which were tied onto the bend of the hook. This turned out to be an insurmountable flaw in the design. One fly per difficult trout might be a reasonable quid pro quo, were the fly not so aggravating and time-consuming to tie.

All in all, I decided that the BW Parachute was a noble—but impractical—effort.

2. The Keel Dun—Under the bucktails in the bottom drawer of my tying desk I discovered an ancient packet of size 14 light-wire hooks made by the Keel Fly Company of Traverse City, Michigan. I had no idea where they came from or how long they had been there but I was inspired. Keel hooks are shaped so that gravity makes them land

upside down—that is, with the point of the hook on top. No need to worry about aerodynamics.

They made deliciously lifelike flies and tying them was easy. First I clamped the hook in the vise in the conventional way, with the hook point down, and tied in the tail. Then I removed the hook, clamped it in upside down, and finished the fly like a conventional Catskill dun, mounting the wings where the hook straightened to the eye. To make it float just right on the water, I clipped a V from the bottom of the hackles.

Nice. Except the Keel Fly Company hooks ran about two sizes bigger than they were marked and all the extra iron made the flies poor floaters. Moreover, in trout sizes, the keel design obstructed the bite, resulting in a ridiculously low percentage of solid hookups.

Still, I could work around the floatation problem, I could compensate for the inaccurately marked sizes, and I could improve the bite on my flies by offsetting the bend.

The Keel Dun. This was it.

I called Information so I could order more hooks. Sorry. No Keel Fly Company listed in Traverse City, Michigan. No forwarding number. As far as I could learn, the Keel Fly Company no longer existed.

The entire Mustad catalog—a tome as thick as my local phone book—listed keel hooks only in saltwater sizes. Tiemco's 205BL, a caddis pupa hook, theoretically did ride with its point up but its odd shape and excessive weight make it unsuitable for dry flies.

Maybe somebody somewhere makes a dry-fly keel hook. But I have found no evidence of it, either by calling fly shops or by scouring the advertisements in magazines.

I was undaunted. I could make my own keel hooks with

two pairs of needle-nose pliers. I broke several hooks before I discovered that by heating the shank over a candle, I could rather easily bend a standard dry-fly hook into a keel shape. Because the two extra bends shortened the finished fly, I used size 12 hooks for size 14 flies and offset the bend to improve the bite.

Hand-making keel hooks, however, was unacceptably time-consuming and fussy. Moreover, I found it practically impossible to reshape hooks smaller than size 12, which eliminated virtually all of the actual flies I wanted to imitate.

Anyway, the Keel Dun always felt vaguely like a cheat.

3. The Backwards Upside Down (BWUSD) Dun—The lifelike elegance of the Clarke and Goddard USD Paradun continued to haunt me. I reconsidered my first effort at an aerodynamic design, the Backwards Parachute. It had consistently floated upside down and it had proved to be a good trout deceiver. It was just too fragile and difficult to tie.

Both of its shortcomings resulted from tying the wings and hackle onto the bend of the hook. But I was convinced that its backwardness maximized the effectiveness of its aerodynamics. I liked the tippet-as-tail feature of it, too.

The trick, I decided, was to design a backwards parachute with the wings and hackle mounted toward the rear—but not directly on the bend—of the hook. It was easy to visualize the finished fly. The wings would flare up on either side of the hook's point and the hackle would be wound around their base.

When I clamped a hook in my vise, however, I realized that winding a parachute hackle as I had imagined it was physically impossible. The bend of the hook got in the way.

I resolved this problem by winding the hackle around the hook itself, then trimming it flush with the top of the shank (which, when it was upside down, would be the bottom of the fly). The result was a fan of hackle that formed a half-circle around the wings and the bend of the hook. I wound forward and tied in a bunch of hackle fibers for a tail so that they flared slightly upwards (in the same direction as the wings), then dubbed the body.

Working thread, wings, and hackle so tight to the point of the hook has produced some frustration. Frayed and broken thread, more times than not. But the finished fly looks so good, I can live with the extra time and care it takes to make.

When I drop one in the bathtub, its aerodynamics make the BWUSD Dun alight with its wings and hook bend up—every time. It perches there on its hackles, remarkably lifelike to my eye.

Come summer, we'll see what the trout say about it, although at this point catching fish on the thing is hardly relevant.

CHAPTER TWENTY-FOUR

FLYMPHS RECONSIDERED

In the 1971 edition of James E. Leisenring's 1941 classic *The Art of Tying the Wet Fly,* Vernon S. Hidy added a few chapters in which he introduced the angling world to the flymph. Half nymph and half wet fly, the flymph imitated "that dramatic and little-understood interval of an aquatic insect's life: the struggle up to the surface as well as the drift (of some insects) in or just below the surface film."

The term "flymph" passed out of our angling lexicon without ever really catching on. But Hidy's astute identification of this important stage of the insect's life cycle—which we now call the "emerger"—sparked a booming little industry of specialized fly patterns and angling strategies.

The fly that Hidy used to imitate the flymph was a simple, wingless hackled fly. Nowadays it's called a "soft-hackled wet fly," although that's something of a misnomer. Anglers who fish with the

Soft Hackle these days generally tie it and use it as an attractor pattern rather than to imitate an emerger (although the trout might think differently when they see it).

Hidy's flymph is basically a soft-hackle wet fly tied in sizes, shapes, and colors to match the insects that are in and on the water. As he described it, the flymph is "a wingless artificial fly with a soft, translucent body of fur or wool which blends with the undercolor of the tying silk when wet, utilizing soft hackle fibers easily activated by the currents to give the effect of an insect alive in the water."

The flymph, and the method Hidy used to fish it, imitated the emerger. He advised anglers to cast "upstream or across for the trout to take just below or within a few inches of the surface film . . . to simulate the hatching nymphs of the mayfly, caddis fly, or other aquatic insects as they struggle up toward the surface or drift momentarily in or just under the surface film."

Despite all the attention that emergers and their imitations have received in the past few decades, references to the soft-hackle (or the flymph) as an effective imitation are rare. For example, Doug Swisher and Carl Richards, in their important book *Emergers* (1991), provide an encyclopedia of lore on this stage of the insect's life. The authors give recipes and tying instructions for dozens of emerger patterns—and never even mention the Soft Hackle or the flymph or Vernon S. Hidy.

If the flymph were merely an historical oddity, Swisher and Richards might be excused. But flymphs work. In my experience, in fact, they usually work better than the fancier (and fussier-to-tie) emerger imitations that Swisher and Richards and others have invented.

Flymphs catch fish throughout the various stages of the hatch—when nymphs first begin to rise to the top of the water, when the half-hatched insects drift in and just under the surface film, when duns (and cripples and stillborns) float on the water, and even when spent and dying spinners ride the downstream currents.

- In the first stage of the emergence, mayfly nymphs, caddis, and midge pupae break away from the river bottom and begin to swim toward the surface, sometimes quite rapidly. Their legs and gills pulsate and vibrate with their efforts. Many never reach the surface, because nearby trout, whose appetites are activated by the appearance of the nymphs, gobble them.

  Dead-drifted nymph or pupa imitations will take some of these trout. But a flymph, fished to imitate the behavior of the insects, works better. "Big Jim" Leisenring special-ized in catching these trout with wet flies. Although he didn't call the wet flies he used "flymphs" (his friend Vernon Hidy hadn't yet coined the term in 1941), Leisenring preferred wingless, soft-hackled wet flies. "I could always, and still can, catch more fish on a wingless imitation," he wrote.

  He cast his flymph upstream of a feeding trout, let it sink to the bottom and drift toward the fish, and as it came within the trout's vision, he "made it to appear alive and escaping" by stopping his rod, which had been following the progress of the fly, causing the fly to rise toward the surface. "The pressure of the water against the stationary line and leader," he wrote, ". . . causes the fly to rise slowly, opening and shutting the hackles, giv-ing a breathing effect such as a genuine insect would have when leaving the bottom of the stream to come to the surface."

- When the nymphs or pupae are near the surface but have not yet begun to metamorphose into duns, the classic tight-line, down-and-across wet-fly swing can be deadly. Fish your flymph this way and trout will hit it violently. The challenge is to avoid having your rod yanked from your hand or snapping your leader. Steer the flymph to the fish with your rod raised and be ready. The strike is usually visible—a splash or bulge or quick flash in the water—and when you see it, you should instantly lower your rod. The tension of the line in the water will cause the trout to hook himself.

• The flymph is absolutely deadly during that time when the nymphs or pupae have reached the surface and are struggling to extricate themselves from their shucks. This is the stage that Hidy specifically targeted with the flymph. He called them "nymphs-about-to-be-born-into-flies"— what we now call "emergers." They drift in or just under the surface film, and with their desperately wiggling legs, their writhing bodies, their bursting wingcases, and their split and dangling shucks, they are shapeless and messy and vulnerable, and no two of them look precisely alike. For this stage, elegant and precise emerger patterns might imitate ten percent of the insects that are in the water. But the suggestive flymph, in the right size and color, represents them all.

You can determine whether this mid-stage insect is on top of the water or trapped in the film or drifting an inch or two under it by studying the riseforms of the feeding trout. Bulges and head-and-shoulder rises mean that they're taking insects beneath the surface. A flymph, fished on a fine tippet and a floating line, will naturally drift at this level.

When trout leave a bubble on the surface, it's likely they're eating floating emergers. Blow your flymph dry and dress it with dry-fly floatant, and it will drift low on the surface film where these trout are feeding.

Whether they're eating off the top or just under the surface, fish the flymph as you would a dry fly. Cast it upstream of a feeding trout and let it dead-drift over him or fish it down-and-across with a reach cast. In either case, the water will cause the hackles to pulsate in a lifelike manner, although adding a slight twitch as the fly approaches a cautious fish might help him to make up his mind.

- When the trout start eating the fully hatched insects that are drifting on tippy-toes on the surface, it's time to switch to a dry fly, right? Well, sure. But if those trout are picky—as they so often are—the flymph can be your problem-solver. Even when they're feeding selectively on floaters, trout can't resist a cripple or a straggling, incompletely hatched nymph or pupa. These insects, trout seem to sense, won't suddenly fly off the way healthy, fully hatched duns and adults tend to do. A flymph in the right color and size, dressed with floatant and fished with a dead drift in the film, has rescued me from many frustrating situations when the trout ignored my high-floating dry fly.

- Trout can be agonizingly selective when they're picking off spent, lifeless spinners. They eat spinners leisurely, knowing that they're not going anywhere, and they take their time to study them. Perfect imitations, cast precisely and fished with no drag whatsoever, will usually catch at least a few of them.

Surprisingly, the suggestive flymph often works better. Fished on the surface, perhaps the flymph suggests a mangled, broken-winged spinner. Trout are always suckers for cripples, even dead ones. Fished an inch or so under the surface, the flymph probably represents a spinner that has been churned and tumbled in the riffles, lost its surface tension, and sunk.

I like the term "flymph" to distinguish these flies from attractor wet flies, both winged and wingless, and from generic Soft Hackles. Flymphs are not complicated to tie. A few wisps of hackle fibers for a tail, a dubbed body, a gold rib, and a couple turns of hackle, that's all. But remember: Flymphs are intended to imitate specific insects and they should be tied with that in mind.

The key to precise imitation is the insect's body. "My experience has taught me," Leisenring wrote, "that bodies of artificial flies are most deadly when, in addition to color, they imitate the texture, translucence, and flash of the natural fly as nearly as possible."

For example, if you're fishing the early stage of a blue-winged olive hatch, when those little dark nymphs are darting and wiggling toward the surface, a properly sized flymph with a pheasant-tail body and a fine gold rib does the job. Later in the emergence, when the naturals have broken out of their nymphal shucks, switch to a dubbed-body flymph the color of the dun.

For the right shape and translucence, dub your flymph bodies sparsely and make them slender. A fine gold or copper rib gives some flash and suggests the segmentation of the natural insect.

Mayfly emergers come with tails and so should your flymphs. Caddis and midge pupae have no tails, of course.

For most situations, the best hackles for a flymph are the breast and side feathers from a game bird such as a grouse or a woodcock. These are the feathers that gave the Soft Hackle its name. Strip the fibers off one side of the feather and tie it in by the tip with the shiny side facing forward. For flies sizes 16 and smaller, wind it just two turns around the front of the fly. For larger flies, three or four turns give the flymph proper balance.

For fishing a flymph with a "Leisenring lift" or across-and-down on a tight line, hackles stiffer than those from game birds work better. The soft hackles tend to collapse around the fly, reducing its lifelike appearance. Carry a selection of flymphs tied with stiffer hen and cock hackles for these situations.

"Future anglers," Vernon Hidy wrote in 1971, "may well consider the three-dimensional flymph technique as more exciting than the dry since it requires a keener observation, greater finesse, and a more delicate touch at the fly-tying table and on the stream."

Hidy was right and he was wrong about us "future anglers." Most of us have incorporated into our arsenal of trout tactics his wisdom about the important emerger stage in the life of aquatic insects. But few of us remember the word he coined for it or the fly he used to imitate it.

It's time we reconsidered the flymph.

CHAPTER TWENTY-FIVE

THE CALCASIEU PIG BOAT

S pinning reels, bass boats, fish-finders, plastic baits, and other high-tech bass-catching equipment arrived in Tom Nixon's part of Louisiana shortly after World War II but he stuck to the fly rod. Not that he was a grumpy old traditionalist or any kind of fly-rod snob. "All I owned were a couple fly rods," he recalls, "and I couldn't really afford new gear. Anyway, I'd always done okay with flies and I can be pretty stubborn."

Nixon wanted to catch bass as much as the next guy, though, and he didn't like getting outfished by his high-tech friends. "I was having to put up with a lot of guff from some of my heave-and-crank acquaintances about fly-rod bass," he remembered, ". . . I was looking hard for something more productive to hang on my leader than the conventional fly baits of the time."

In 1951 Nixon responded to this challenge by inventing the Calcasieu Pig Boat, which was inspired by the Hawaiian Wiggler, a popular postwar rubber-legged bait-casting lure. The Pig Boat resembled no "fly" anyone had ever seen. He named it after the Calcasieu River, his home bass water in southwestern Louisiana. The fly proved lethal on bass. Nixon likened it to a German submarine, which, he said, was "a deadly underwater predator" known during the war as a "pig boat."

In fact, Tom Nixon's Pig Boat should properly be regarded as nothing less than a revolutionary creation, a transitional design that liberated fly-rod bass fishing from the limitations of surface fishing with bugs and made it a legitimate sport for all water types and conditions. "Far too many capable and dedicated fishermen had wedded their fly rods to the cork-body popping bug," he wrote, "and when this combination failed to produce, they called it a day and went home."

The Pig Boat's most prominent feature—dozens of wiggly rubber legs entirely encircling the hook—makes it more of a lure than a fly. It was the first bass "bait" specifically designed to be cast and fished with the fly rod. Its body resembles a Woolly Worm—heavy black chenille wound over with thickly palmered grizzly hackle. What makes it a Pig Boat are fifty-six to seventy-two strands of thin black rubber thread that are tied as a collar in front.

In your hand, a Pig Boat looks like a mating cluster of tarantulas. In the water, it wiggles and shimmies in ways that bass—and, in fact, most species of fish—cannot resist.

In 1954 Harold F. Blaisdell's *Field & Stream* story "Pig Boat on the Furnace" brought Nixon and his creation national attention. Blaisdell suspected that the Pig Boat would make an enticing mouthful for big predatory brown trout and he proved it one evening on Furnace Brook, his local Vermont trout stream. "What puzzled me," recalled Nixon tongue-in-cheekly, "was why anyone would waste a good bass bait on brown trout. . . Mr. Blaisdell received a good bass bait and promptly let some old brown trout slobber all over it."

The original black-and-grizzly Pig Boat worked great most of the time. But Nixon didn't stop there. Wrapping lead wire around the hook shank sank it down to water levels where bass sometimes lurked out of reach of an unweighted version. Clamping a spinner ahead of it added bass-attracting flash in murky water. Rigging it with an offset spinner converted the Pig Boat into a deadly fly-rod spinnerbait, while a six-inch plastic worm split in half and trailed behind a Pig Boat made a lethal bass lure. When he discovered that impaling a pork rind on the hook sometimes caught more bass than an unfettered Pig Boat, Nixon tied in a sprig of white rubber thread as a pork-rind substitute and called it a "Sproat Boat."

He made them in different colors and sizes, and varied his retrieves according to weather and water conditions—deep and slow, fast and shallow, and even dead-drifted in lazy southern river currents.

The effectiveness of his Pig Boat encouraged Nixon to experiment by fly casting with spin-fishing bass baits such as plastic worms, jig-and-pigs, and spinnerbaits. And then he devised "flies" that worked as well. In the process, he showed the way for present-day fly-rod bass gurus, who no longer restrict themselves to floating bugs and whose repertoire of skills, tactics, and lures rivals that of the bass-tournament fishermen.

"A bass," Nixon wrote, "is a far cry from the conventional target of the long rod. So, when the conventional concepts of tackle, lures, and procedures fail to interest an unconventional quarry, go it his way."

Which is not to say that Tom Nixon ever turned up his nose at "conventional" flies. In fact, he invented dozens of more or less conventional flies and bugs and adapted countless old standards for southern largemouths and bream. All of them are proven fish-takers. He gave some of them delightful Cajun names—Sowela, Phideaux, Zeeke, Zombola, Maziere, Emida. Other names just seem to fit— Poofy, Big Sister, Shifty, Dog, Butcher.

My personal favorite Nixon fly name is the .56%er. It's a little weighted gray-and-yellow trout nymph that is also deadly for Cajun—and New England—bluegills. Nixon observed that no trout dry-fly purist is really 100 percent pure. "A thorough analysis," he noted slyly, "shows 99.44% to be the maximum degree of purity attainable, but they are 100% fishermen. . . . This scrawny-looking misfit of a fly was offered and accepted because no one could possibly blame a guy for trying one out in the upstream riffle."

Twenty-five years ago, when a local bass club invited Tom Nixon to participate in their tournaments on the Toledo Bend Reservoir on the Texas-Louisiana border, he accepted the chance to stack his fly rod up against their spinning and bait-casting gear. He entered five tournaments. "Got one first, one second, and two thirds," he recalled. "The other one I got disqualified. We were camping out and the alarm didn't go off. Slept through the start." He caught all of his tournament bass on two flies—most of them on a spinner-and-Pig-Boat rig ("for underwater") and a few on a yellow cork popping bug ("when I found 'em on top").

Tom Nixon was never much for philosophizing. But his love of fly tying and fly fishing for bass bubbled forth from both his conversation and his writing. "The easy grace of a fly rod," he wrote in 1977, "the thrill it affords in playing and landing a fish, the casting accuracy that is accomplished, all of these things make the long rod one of the most sporting and pleasant ways to fish for bass."

Shortly before he died in 2003, Nixon published a new edition of his classic book *Fly Tying and Fly Fishing for Bass and Panfish,* which first appeared in 1968 and was last updated in 1977. He was also writing a memoir called *50 Years of Warmwater Fly Fishing.*

Right up to the time he died at the age of ninety, Nixon fished on his Louisiana bass rivers for an hour or two just about every day.

The last time I talked to him, I asked what luck he'd had that morning. In that soft Cajun drawl of his, Tom said, "Oh, I got some on a Pig Boat. I usually do."

CHAPTER TWENTY-SIX

◄══◆══►

TAP'S BUG

In the beginning, Ernest H. Peckinpaugh created the Night Bug. The beginning, for our purposes, came sometime shortly after the turn of the last century, and the Night Bug was a cork-bodied bucktail streamer tied on a double hook. Peckinpaugh's bugs took Tennessee bream toward evening when they began to "spat" for insects on the surface of his local ponds. When he discovered that largemouth bass were attracted to Night Bugs, he began to tie them on larger hooks. Thus was born surface fishing for bass with the fly rod.

When the Great War cut off Peckinpaugh's supply of double hooks, he adapted his creation to the single hook. Sometime in the 1920s, Will H. Dilg of Chicago happened upon the Night Bug. Dilg experimented with a variety of designs, and his magazine articles popularized the sport of bass-bug fishing with cork-bodied poppers and the fly rod.

Soon thereafter the magical properties of deerhair were discovered. Spun tightly onto a hook and trimmed to shape, deerhair floated—well, like a cork. Fly tiers, probably feeling that carving and gluing cork qualified more as cabinetmaking than fly tying, adapted deer hair to bass-bug design. Early deerhair bugs were aerodynamic disasters that required heavy tackle and powerful shoulders to cast. But they glugged and gurgled on the surface and bass crashed them.

Design refinements came quickly. The Calmac Moth moved quietly on the water's surface suggesting a large insect. Joe Messinger designed his elegant and still-popular Hair Frog, and Roy Yates invented the muddler-like Deacon.

They all, of course, caught bass. But none quite satisfied my father. Neither the cork-body bugs nor the bulky deerhair designs, which typically came with outrigger wings and big feather-duster tails, were pleasant to cast. The moth variations didn't make the surface disturbance that Dad thought attracted predatory bass. Tying Messinger frogs was fussy and time-consuming—and when he made a good one, he considered it too beautiful to fish with.

"Until Roy Yates sent me one of his Deacons," he said, "I mostly used a bait-casting rod and Jitterbugs or Magic Minnows for bass on the surface. The Deacon converted me to fly-rod bass bugging, mainly because I found I could cast it comfortably on a five- or six-weight trout rod. I caught a lot of bass on the Deacon. But I kept wondering how I could improve it."

My father made a career out of inventing and refining and simplifying. For thirty-five years he shared his thoughts and creations in his "Tap's Tips" column for *Field & Stream,* and I can report from extensive personal experience that he was a compulsive tinkerer. In fact, in 1946 he wrote a book called *Tackle Tinkering* (the title— *Tinkle Tackering* by H. G. Tipply . . . no, that's not it . . . inspired one of Ed Zern's most hilarious columns).

"The best feature of the Deacon," said Dad, "was its streamlined shape. It cast as comfortably as a streamer fly. But I felt it didn't kick up enough of a fuss on the surface due to its little round head. And there wasn't enough clipped deerhair on it to keep it afloat very long. So I began experimenting."

His early efforts featured a full-length clipped deerhair body with a flat bottom and a wide rounded front end tapered to a point at the rear. He left whiskers at the head and made a tail of flared hackle feathers. "I soon cut off those whiskers," he said. "Too air-resistant for pleasant casting, and they tended to twist the leader and make the thing land upside down. To get the kind of burble I wanted, I left the face flat rather than rounding it off. I fiddled with the tail. The hackle feathers gave it a nice leggy action but they made the thing whistle and spin when I cast it. I tried bucktail but getting a nice smooth transition from the tail into the deerhair body was difficult. Finally I found some long deer body hair that worked beautifully for the tail. I tie it in right at the butts and they flare to form the beginning of the body. If there's any secret to tying one of these things, it's using the right deerhair for the tail. It's got to be hollow at the butt ends, and it should be long and fine at the tips so the tail end of it doesn't flare too much. All the rest is spinning and packing and hedge-trimming the deerhair. It's kind of fun. I can make one in about twenty minutes."

I watched my father tie his bugs since I was old enough to climb onto his lap and make half hitches, and although he always kept me well supplied with Tap's Bugs (as he did dozens of fly-casting bass fishermen across the country), I've tied plenty of them myself. Next to his beautifully symmetrical creations, mine tend to look misshapen and amateurish. But the bass do not seem to discriminate.

Besides finding the right hair for the tail, the only "trick" to making one of Tap's Bugs is to get that flared deerhair packed densely onto the bare hook shank. Dad spun on a drinking straw-sized bundle, tied it off with a half-hitch, and then, pinching the base of the tail tightly between his left thumb and forefinger, he used his right thumb and forefinger to twist and push the flared hair back. "Don't be gentle with it," he advised. "Use strong thread. You want that deerhair compressed as tight as you can get it. I feel that I can cram it tighter with my fingers than with a packing tool. The denser it is, the neater it will be when you trim it and the longer your bug will float."

The flat face, Dad believed, made all the difference in his bug's behavior. "It doesn't pop," he said. "I always felt a loud pop such as you get from some hard-bodied bugs is just as likely to spook a bass as attract him. But a flat-faced deerhair bug plows through the water and burbles when you twitch and retrieve it, and it seems to drive bass nuts. I believe, though I couldn't prove it, that bass are less likely to spit out a soft lifelike deerhair bug than a hard-bodied cork or balsa popper."

Back in the 1970s Dad sent some of his bugs to his outdoor-writing colleague Charles Waterman. The author of *Fly Rodding for Bass* wrote back: "Last week we used your bugs, together with poppers, on Lake Okeechobee, and yours were winners by a considerable margin." Others who've tried them report similar results.

Dad tied his bugs on 2/0 hooks for largemouths and No. 1 hooks for smallmouths. Color? "I like yellow or white simply because I can see it better," he said, "and when I make 'em in other colors I often put some white or yellow at the face for the same reason. But natural gray works fine. Charley Waterman says that in his experience all white seems to work best for smallmouths. Personally, I doubt that color makes a bit of difference to the fish."

But besides being a tinkerer, Dad also had a streak of the artist in him, so a box of Tap-tied bugs always contained many combinations of red, green, yellow, orange, white, and black. By alternating colors as he spun on the dyed hair, he produced striped effects. He mingled yellow and green in ways that gave his bugs a frog-like appearance, and yellow and black looked a lot like a bumblebee. "But these things don't imitate anything," he insisted. "I fool around with color combinations just for the fun of it. Make 'em glug and gurgle so they act like something alive and vulnerable. It's the burble that triggers strikes, not the color."

Dad kept his rod tip pointing at the bug and retrieved it by tugging at the line rather than lifting his rod. After a few casts, the deer-hair absorbed some water and rode lower. This actually enhanced the burble. When the bug beccame waterlogged, as it eventually did, he simply squeezed the water out of it and resumed casting.

"I look for flat water and shade," he said. "I think bass are reluctant to strike surface lures or flies in the bright sun, and too much ripple neutralizes the fish-attracting commotion of the bug. Early morning and evening, sheltered shores, soft cloudy days with maybe a little mist falling—those are bass-bugging conditions."

A six-weight fly rod loaded with a weight-forward (bass-bug taper) floating line and an eight-foot leader tapered to about 1X makes the ideal outfit for casting Tap's Bugs.

Dad always crimped down the barbs on his bugs. "I never keep bass," he said, "and they sometimes inhale the bug and get it deep—especially the smallmouths, for some reason. When they get it in their throats, I just cut the leader and let them keep the bug."

I grew up fishing with my father for both largemouths and smallmouths all over New England. Tap's Bug is about all I've ever used when surface fishing for bass, and lately I've found that it works equally well for schoolie stripers. Miniature bugs are ideal for bluegills. Pickerel and northern pike and bluefish crash big long-tailed versions (although it doesn't take many of those toothy critters to shred a bug). Once in Labrador, a five-pound brook trout pounced on the pike-sized bug I was glugging through some lily pads.

I've enjoyed casting Dad's aerodynamic bug almost as much as catching bass on it. A good bass shore offers an infinite variety of targets. Here I drop the bug at the base of a stump or into a pocket among lily pads. Next I throw a hard, tight sidearm loop and skip it under overhanging brush into a dark hole against the bank. I drive it under a dock or bounce it off a boulder. Then I plop it among the dead limbs of a fallen tree. I crawl it back. It burbles. It rests. It twitches and glugs across the water's still surface.

And no matter how tense and expectant I am, the sudden boil that engulfs my bug never fails to startle me.

CHAPTER TWENTY-SEVEN

THE NEARENUF

For thirty-five years—from 1950 to 1985—my father filled two pages of *Field & Stream* with useful information for outdoorsmen. There were the fifty-word "Tap's Tips"—six every month—for which Tap's name became famous, and there were the five-hundred-word "Sportsman's Notebook" articles—one per month, and for a while, two—that needed the extra words to explain more complicated things.

I've done the math. More than twenty-five hundred Tips and four hundred and fifty Notebooks. That adds up to about one hundred new and useful ideas each year and over one-third of a million words—and not a single one wasted—in thirty-five years.

What most people didn't realize but what I, his son, understood, is that for every Tip-worthy idea that Dad selected to write about, he discarded three as impractical or unhelpful or just plain dumb. He field-tested everything exhaustively and I got to go along and "help" him.

We had to do a lot of fishing and hunting to test one hundred ideas a year. Lucky me.

Sometime in the 1950s when I was a young teenager, with the trout season upon us, Dad gave me a box of dry flies. "I need your help," he said.

I opened the box. Except for their sizes, which ranged from 12 to 18, every fly was identical. I arched my eyebrows at him.

"Here's the idea," he said, in pretty much the same words he used a few years later when he felt confident enough to write about it. "If I'm right, this should be the only dry fly we'll ever need. With this range of sizes, and relieved of the worry about what pattern we should tie on, we can concentrate on the important matter of fishing the fly properly. We've just got to figure out if I'm right."

I picked up one of the flies and held it in the palm of my hand. It had a split wood-duck flank-feather wing, mixed ginger-and-grizzly hackle, a stripped peacock quill body, and a pair of stripped grizzly quills, splayed wide, for tails. It reminded me a little bit of many dry fly patterns we used but it was identical to none of them.

"What do you call it?" I said.

He shrugged. "I don't know. It doesn't have a name. It's a mongrel. I've tried to blend the elements of our common eastern mayfly hatches—Quill Gordon, Red Quill, Hendrickson, March Brown, Gray Fox, Light Cahill, Pale Evening Dun. It doesn't really imitate any of them, as you can see. But if I'm right, we should discover that it's near enough."

And that's what he eventually called it: the Nearenuf.

Several of Dad's trout-fishing friends agreed to participate in his experiment in exchange for a season's supply of Tap-tied flies, and for two full seasons of dry-fly fishing, all of us used only the Nearenuf regardless of what was hatching.

At the end of the second season, Dad insisted on candid reports from all participants. None of us felt that we'd been handicapped in the slightest or had caught fewer trout using the Nearenuf than in previous years when we'd attempted to match the hatches precisely. We'd spent more time stalking trout, making accurate casts, and achieving drag-free floats, and we'd wasted less time poking our noses into our fly boxes. As Dad wrote: "If you use the Nearenuf, your only problem will be to match the size of the hatching flies, a much simpler matter than trying first to identify whatever those things are that are dancing over the water, and then to match them in both pattern and size, which generally involves much fumble-fingered tying on and snipping off of flies the fish don't seem to want."

Dad never claimed that the Nearenuf was a magic fly. That wasn't his point. He didn't believe in magic flies. He believed that presentation was more important than imitation, and he admitted that for all he knew, an Adams or a Quill Gordon, if fished properly, would catch as many trout during any mayfly hatch as a Nearenuf.

There are many times when trout are not eating mayfly duns. On those occasions, a small pair of sharp scissors and a Nearenuf of the right size will still do the job of several boxes of patterns.

- If you find trout feeding on low-riding duns in flat, slow-moving water, you can improve a Nearenuf by clipping a V out of the bottom of the hackle.
- If they're eating emergers in the film, cut the bottom hackle flat and trim down the wings.
- If they're sipping spinners, clip the hackle flat on the bottom, cut off the wings, and clip a V out of the top of the hackle.
- If they're gobbling nymphs in or near the surface film, cut the hackle and wings to a nub. Spit on it to make it sink.

- If they're targeting cripples, cut the bottom of the hackle at an angle and amputate one wing.

With a little creative barbering, Tap's Nearenuf comes awfully close to fulfilling the promise implied by the title of the article he eventually wrote about it: "One Fly for Every Hatch."

I don't know anybody who literally fishes with just one fly. I certainly don't. Dad's point was that you would handicap yourself less than you might expect if you focused your attention on variables other than fly pattern.

I think he was right.

EPILOGUE

GONE FISHIN'

We usually rumble across the iron bridge, turn off the road, follow the bumpy ruts beside the field, and park Dad's wagon at the water's edge to offload the canoe, but on this gray afternoon in January we've come in my car and we have to leave it beside the road and slog through knee-deep snow to the stream.

Today we leave the rods in the car. We haven't bothered with the canoe.

I brush the snow off a boulder beside the water for Dad, then perch on my own rock next to him.

"Looks kinda different in the winter, huh?" he says.

The black currents flow against the crusty ice along the banks and swirl slowly around the bridge abutments. The alders and willows are black and skeletal against the snow. The sky overhead is leaden. The winter air carries the taste of more snow.

"No mayflies today," I offer.

Dad laughs quietly. "I can count the mayfly hatches we've encountered here on the fingers of one hand. Objectively, it's not much of a trout stream."

"But we do love it," I say.

"That we do," he says softly.

We've been coming to this little stream for nearly forty years. We discovered it soon after Dad moved to New Hampshire, and over the years we've explored its entire twenty-odd miles. It empties a spring-fed trout pond, meanders through pine-and-hardwood forest, opens up for a couple of miles in a bog, and reenters the forest before it dumps into the lake. We know every pool and run and riffle, every eddy and backwater and hole, and I guess at one time or another we've caught trout from all of them. We've been skunked plenty of times, too. We've packed away a lot of memories here.

We've always come with the same purpose: To have some time with each other. Sharing a canoe on a quiet woodland trout stream for an afternoon, taking turns paddling and casting, has been our way of staying connected. The fishing is quite secondary, although before today we never considered leaving our fly rods behind.

It's a wild, pretty little stream, mayflies or no mayflies. In June the cardinal flowers and wild irises and marigolds splash patches of color over the banks, and in the fall the maples form a crimson-and-gold canopy overhead. We've rounded a bend, paddling or push-poling quietly, and found deer and, on a couple of occasions, a moose standing in the shallows. Kingfishers and herons hunt trout here, and in the fall migrating warblers swarm in the bushes. We've flushed wood ducks and blacks and mallards. We've always planned to come back in October for a shotgun-and-fly-rod float but grouse season has inevitably distracted us.

What we've liked best of all about our stream is its inaccessibility. Just two bridges cross it—this iron bridge at about the halfway mark and the highway bridge near its terminus. Its brush-clogged mud banks and silty bottom make it impossible to wade or fish from shore. The only way is from a little canoe, the way we've always done it. There are rocky riffles that in low-water years we've had to drag over. Enough uprooted pines lie across the water to discourage recreational canoeists and kayakers. They have never discouraged us.

We're thankful that our stream does not appear on the state's list of stocked waters. The New England brook trout that live here were either born in one of its tiny tributaries or have wandered up or down from the ponds at either end.

Except for the occasional kid dangling a worm from one of the bridges, in forty years we have never encountered another fisherman here.

Dad and I sit there beside each other, watching the dark January water flow past us. Forty years, a hundred trips, at least. I'm having vague thoughts of immortality and eternity, thoughts that swirl in my mind like the black currents in our stream, elusive, opaque thoughts I can't quite sink a hook into. Past, present, and future mingle, the river and the memories . . .

It's a sunny Saturday in May, or maybe June or September. I've driven to New Hampshire to spend some time with my father. His wagon is parked in the driveway. He's already strapped on the canoe, packed corned-beef sandwiches and bottles of Hires root beer in the basket, stowed the fishing gear. He's waiting for me in the yard, pretending to be busy weeding a flower garden or repairing a birdfeeder. When I pull in, he looks up, waves, glances at his watch. I'm early. I've been looking forward to this all week. He has, too, I know.

A half hour later we cross the iron bridge. We offload the canoe, stow the gear, rig the rods. We argue about who will start in the bow with the rod and who will paddle. It's an argument I have never won. Dad always asserts his seniority and takes the stern seat.

He pushes us upstream. I sit up front and scan the water for the dimple of a rising trout. Now and then he digs in his paddle and holds the canoe. He says nothing but after all these years, no words are needed. I know he wants me to drift my bushy dry fly through that current seam or along that shaded undercut bank or against that boulder. We both remember a time when we took a trout there.

Where the stream meanders through the bog, Dad grabs a branch to hold us still. "Listen," he whispers.

It's the weird, booming "pump-er-lunk" call of the bittern, a haunting, wild sound that never fails to make me shiver, a sound I will forever associate with our stream, with Dad. It sounds close and we look hard. But as often as we've heard Mr. Bittern, we've never once been able to spot him.

After a couple of hours we beach the canoe and sit on a sunny patch of grass with the picnic basket between us. We discuss baseball, politics, religion, economics. We disagree on a lot of things. I call him a stubborn old Yankee. He calls me a crazy Communist. We like to debate. But we never argue. We listen to each other and we learn from each other.

When the sandwiches and root beer are gone, we lie back on the grass. We listen to the music of the birds and the water, and we gaze up through the lacy tree branches to the sky, and it's easy to wind back through the years to all the other times Dad and I have been together at this stream, or at some other stream. It never mattered where we were or whether we caught many trout. Time and place were irrelevant as long as we shared them.

Dad murmurs, "It's good to get out, isn't it?"

"Yes," I say quietly. "It's always good to get out."

After a while, he stands up and stretches. "Let's go catch some trout." He tries to take the paddle.

I grab it from him. "My turn," I say.

"I'd rather paddle."

"So would I. Don't be selfish."

He grumbles, of course, but he takes the bow seat and picks up the rod. We've done this a hundred times. We both love to fish.

We drift downstream. Dad roll-casts his little bucktail against the bank. He's as effortless and graceful and accurate as ever. Watching him from behind, I can almost convince myself that nothing has changed in forty years, that the stream will always be here, and we will, too . . .

"You must be getting cold," Dad says.

"You taught me not to complain," I reply. "How about you?"

"Ha, ha," he says. "Very funny."

Hard little snowflakes are spitting down from the low January sky. I haven't noticed them until just now. "Storm coming," I say.

"Won't bother me," he says. "But maybe it's time."

I nod and stand up. "Okay. It's time."

Dad's ashes swirl and disappear in the dark currents, mingling with our stream and with our memories.

"You're on your own this time," I tell him. I lift my hand. "Tight lines."

Then I turn and trudge across the snow-covered field to my car, on my own myself for the first time in my life.

ABOUT THE AUTHOR

William G. Tapply is the author of more than thirty books, among them twenty-one New England-based Brady Coyne mystery novels. Tapply has written several books about fly fishing and the outdoors, including *Pocket Water* and *Bass Bug Fishing.* He is a contributing editor for *Field & Stream,* a columnist for *American Angler,* and has written hundreds of articles and essays on a variety of subjects for dozens of other publications. Tapply is a professor of English at Clark University in Worcester, Massachusetts, where he teaches writing. He lives in Hancock, New Hampshire, with novelist Vicki Stiefel, his wife, and Burt, his Brittany spaniel.